Page
Bottom poem

molly furtado

fart doo tenly

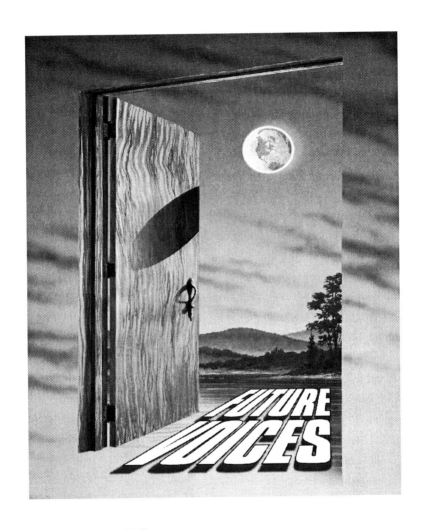

FROM NORTHAMPTONSHIRE

Edited by Dave Thomas

First published in Great Britain in 2000 by
YOUNG WRITERS
Remus House,
Coltsfoot Drive,
Woodston,
Peterborough, PE2 9JX
Telephone (01733) 890066

HB ISBN 0 75431 930 X
SB ISBN 0 75431 931 8

FOREWORD

This year, the Young Writers' Future Voices competition proudly presents a showcase of the best poetic talent from over 42,000 up-and-coming writers nationwide.

Successful in continuing our aim of promoting writing and creativity in children, our regional anthologies give a vivid insight into the thoughts, emotions and experiences of today's younger generation, displaying their inventive writing in its originality.

The thought, effort, imagination and hard work put into each poem impressed us all and again the task of editing proved challenging due to the quality of entries received, but was nevertheless enjoyable. We hope you are as pleased as we are with the final selection and that you continue to enjoy *Future Voices From Northamptonshire* for many years to come.

CONTENTS

Lisa Greenwood	19
Amie Kendall	20
Blayne Patmore	20
Sarah Williams	21
Kerrie Cotman	21
Rebecca Stone	22
Mark Duncan	22
Glen Pierre Roberts	23
Paul Harry	23
Joanne Baxter	24
Victoria Jeffery	24
David Roberts	24
Kim Scriven	25
William Bell	26
Ben Glazier	26
Paul Hancock	27
Barbara Zydonik	27

Daventry William Parker School

Matthew Nicholls	27
Katherine Weller	28
Neil Murray	28
Natalie Bell	29
Hollie Drinkwater	29
Lindsey Thompson	30
Fae Unger	30
Laura Barrell	31
Gemma Bolderson	31
Alison Sargent	31
Susan Joynson	32
Siann Grant	32
Helen Trueman	33
Jenny Cooper	33
Rachael Hopper	34
Sophie Pritchard	35
Melissa Mudge	35
Simon Hudson	36
Samantha Beames	36

Chloe Swingler	83
Lindsay Appleton	84

Manor School

Jade Farrer	84
Adam Kemp	85
Oliver Maitland	85
Gina Heatley	86
Ryan Jones	86
Adele Bulmer	87
Lucy De Friend	88
Alex Ng	89
Oliver Owers-Gibbs	90
Adam Gayton	91
Ben Munns	92
Chris Sinclair	92
Michael Lewis	93
Ashlee Stovold	94
Victoria Commins	94
Kayleigh Manciocchi	95
Emma Saddington	95
Daniel Marsh	96
Tara Damon	96
Jade Wiggins	97

Prince William School

Katie Wilson & Jade Dixon-Winters	98
Raymond Chambers	99
Kirsty Neild	100
Leigh Middleton	100
Louise Coombes	101
Fiona Warren	102
Claire Solesbury	102
Claire Warren	103
Lisa Snoxell	104
Sophie Dall	104
Sophie O'Brien	105
Rachel Dunn	105

Tom Grace	106
James Rudkin	106

Roade School

Philip Costin	107
Megan Boot	108
Hannah Maher	108
Jennifer Gordon	109
Jennifer Duckett	110
Hannah Spotwood	110
Daniel Whitlock	111
Hannah Steele	111
Hayley Creffield	112
Sarah Kennedy	112
Amy Whittle	113
Laura Bradshaw	114
Doug Mackenzie	114
Lee Holod	115
Ryan Oakley	116
Victoria Hayward	116
Abigail Stanbridge	117
Kathryn Johnson	118
Nicola Swinney	118
Christopher Osgood	119
Adam Murby	120
Kelly Lack	120
Gaby Knight	121
Rebecca Hayward	122
Jenna Harrison	123
Hannah Mead	123
Harry Ingram	124
Nicola Powell	124
Harsimran Samrai	125
Sam Desborough	126
Sophie Hillyard	127
Nicky Lloyd	128
Becci Moss	128
Lauren Dyer	129

The Poems

SNOW

Snow is . . .
white,
light,
dinting,
glinting,
slushy,
mushy.

Snow covers . . .
people,
playgrounds,
plants,
panes,
post boxes,
pigeons.

You can . . .
throw it,
stow it,
melt it,
pelt it,
crush it,
mush it.

Snow snows . . .
silently,
smotheringly,
stealthily,
softly,
slowly,
sleepily.

I like snow.

Harriet Vickers (13)

AN OLD MOUSE TAIL!

Silence!
The coast is clear,
But does she dare?
. . . One step,
Don't make a sound!
Scared stiff,
She tiptoes across the wooden floorboards!

MiaowwwwwwWWWWW!
Panic!
She scurries round and round in circles.
She was then in clear sight of the ferocious *cat!*
He opened his colossal mouth,
Showing his sharp teeth
Darkness, followed by . . .
        Silence!

Rebecca Cole (11)
Bishop Stopford School

ANIMALS

A is for animals, who are cute and cuddly
N is for naughty, which most animals are
I is for intelligence, which animals have quite a lot of
M is for mischievous, which represents my animals
A is for active, which all animals should be
L is for lovely, every animal in the world is lovely
S is for super, all animals are absolutely super.

Hannah Welch (11)
Bishop Stopford School

AMERICA TO ENGLAND

It was a cool summer night,
When I had a fight.
Now you wonder why?
It was because I had to fly,
Away from my home,
From everything that tends,
To give me my hope.
How would I cope?
I guess I have to explain,
Why I'm in pain.
I was scheduled to move,
How would I groove? (American)
The next week I reached a peak,
I couldn't stand it any longer.
I soon found out I couldn't be any wronger.
Packing all those things,
Then the doorbell rings,
The movers are here,
Would I dare to peer,
Around the corner?
Now I was a mourner.
They were taking my books,
My pictures and hooks.
Now I'm in school,
Being a fool.
Now I know I was wrong!

Sarah Komline (11)
Bishop Stopford School

CULTURE CARPENTRY

The designers were my parents,
They built my structure,
God did the sawing,
Cutting every bone to perfection.
Teachers did the hammering,
Knocking information into my head.
Society did the sanding,
Rounding off the rough edges.
Family is my glue,
Keeping me strong and complete.
Education was the chisel,
Slowly changing me into an adult.
Vocabulary is my knots,
Making me original and a collector's piece.
The varnish making me shine,
Is my ability to read and write.
Wood cultivation is carpentry.
Human cultivation is culture.

Esther Straub (16)
Bishop Stopford School

THE TIGER

Running past,
Running fast,
Running, jumping,
Four legs pumping.

Tiger, stripy, very stripy,
Running through the trees,
Tiger stripy, very stripy,
Why do you do it?
Tell me please.

Orange and black,
What's that shack?
Home of the country folk -
The ones you never provoke.

Tiger stripy, very stripy,
Running through the trees,
Tiger stripy, very stripy,
Why do you do it?
Tell me please.

Sarah Beasley (12)
Bishop Stopford School

THE ELEPHANT

The elephant's trunk sways and sways
He slowly moves forward, it's been a tiring day.
The rhythm and movement of his huge feet
Makes a steady sound and a musical beat.
He cools himself down with a trunkful of dust
Looking around with patience and trust.
His eyes look cautiously all around
Then he turns his gaze to the ground.
He knows the hunter is somewhere near
He stands completely still and shows no fear.
He holds his majestic head high
And fills the air with a piercing cry.
As the sun shone on his back
The elephant followed his own marked-out track.

Emma Spikesley (11)
Bishop Stopford School

HELLO SIR!

Hello Sir!
What's it today?
What did you say?
Maths and PE?
Have we DT?
Oh, what a shame!
I am a pain,
I've forgotten my book
No I haven't, look!

Oh no, Sir!
My pencil broke.
Polly just spoke.
I didn't hear -
Did you say 'Near?'
I spelt it wrong.
That word's too long.
My pen ran out -
'Oh bother!' I shout.

Lunchtime, Sir!
What have you got?
Is it a lot?
Ham sandwich for me -
The same as Lee.
Would you like one?
Have you got some?
Mmm! That was nice!
My Müller Rice.

Last lesson, Sir!
I do love art.
I think it's smart.
You look so tired -
Hardly inspired.
I like the blue,
Do you like it too?
Hey, that was the bell!
'Home time!' we yell.

Emma Lee (13)
Bishop Stopford School

WHY?

I often sit and wonder why
Why are we here, why oh why?
Why is the sky so big and blue?
And why is the sea as deep as my eye?
Why oh why?

I often sit and wonder why
Why am I me, why oh why?
Why couldn't I have been that person next door?
And why couldn't I have been a bird to fly so high?
Why, oh why?

I often sit and remember now
Why I'm here and how,
I'm here because I'm me and nothing else
I know why, I know now!

Stacey Dunkley (12)
Blackthorn Middle School

A POEM ABOUT A POEM

A poem can be as long as it likes
It can be about anything
It can be about you and your bike
Or how you love to sing.

A poem can be short
And could be about school
All the lessons you have been taught
And all about the rules.

Now I've come to my conclusion
A poem could be anything
It doesn't even have to rhyme
If you don't want it to
You can decide what you put in
And what you write about
All in all a poem is . . .

Tina Winton (12)
Blackthorn Middle School

I WISH I WAS A PROFESSIONAL FOOTBALLER

If I was a professional footballer
I would probably have to be a bit taller.
I would warm-up with all the lads
And during the game I would make the coach glad.
If only I was a professional footballer
I would be a top performer.

Vincent Bloyce (12)
Blackthorn Middle School

NIGHTMARE

A slimy snake, slithering,
A mouldy piece of cheese,
A rabid wolf frothing at the mouth,
An axe murderer swinging for his victim,
12pm midnight on Hallowe'en night,
A street rat scurrying for shelter,
A flea-bitten battered armchair,
A witch's potion, boiling and gurgling,
A mouldy skull rotting with neglect,
A pair of smelly Wellington boots squishing
and squelching in the mud,
A wet and cold October evening
An X-rated horror movie,
A rundown barnyard smothered in graffiti.
Nightmare!

Kelle Reilly (12)
Blackthorn Middle School

LOVE IS . . .

Love is in the air,
Love is what we breathe.
Love is happiness.
Love is when you really like someone.
Love is going out together.
Love is holding hands.
Love is marriage.
Love is happy memories.
Love is a time of joyfulness.

Daniel Perryman (12)
Blackthorn Middle School

THE GOAL

Players wait,
Ref blows for kick-off,
Keane gives a cross,
Beckham receives,
Adams tackles,
Passes to Giggs,
Giggs runs and crosses,
Beckham rushes in,
Gets a header,
Seaman saves,
Yorke with the rebound,
Scores!
The celebrations begin,
Could this be
The goal that counts?

Emily Earl (13)
Blackthorn Middle School

DEATH

Age and a failing lung,
A growing murmur of a once youthful man,
His growing pain,
Death is lurking round every corner,
The day dies and night arrives,
His soul and life being drained away,
I'm miles away and his life is ended,
And the Grim Reaper takes another soul.

Christopher Boaden (12)
Blackthorn Middle School

THE BIZARRE KITCHEN!

Pots and pans on the floor
Lumps of spaghetti thrown at the door.
A bit of apple crumble,
And a bit of cherry pie
I was just about to eat them
When I swore I saw a fly.
I was trying to make some coffee
it was not a success
It got mixed with the toffee
And came out as a mess.
The water in the pan is three days old
The cheese looks horrible
It's covered with mould.
I felt very sick
So ran very quick
I threw up in the basin
And the cat dipped his face in.

Stefanie Ennis (12)
Blackthorn Middle School

ELEPHANT

It always seem to be looking sad and never happy,
Its trunk is always very active.
Its ears and skin are as rough as sandpaper.
Its feet wouldn't stand on an ant (except if it was blind.)
The ground shakes as it moves,
Its ears could make a hurricane.
It has a tail like fly-swats that hurt severely.

Daniel Lee (11)
Blackthorn Middle School

MY SISTER SUSIE

My name is Lucy,
I have a sister called Susie.
She makes me eat her carrots and peas,
And makes me wash the dog when it has fleas.
She's the worst person I've ever known,
And is always off to the bank for a loan.
She's on the phone 24 hours, seven days,
And cannot stop shopping at 'Kays'.
I have to share a room with her,
And her annoying hamster, Clever.
I don't know why she named him that,
She should've named him something like Fat.
Well, there you go, that's my sister Susie,
If you would like to trade sisters . . .
Call me!

Jane Nong (12)
Blackthorn Middle School

LIFE

Life is important and you should try anything you want to do.
Life is a thing that is enjoyable and very, very precious.
Life is an important thing to everyone,
And everyone should take their time
And take life one step at a time.
Life should be your most prized possession
Within the whole world.
And I don't intend in wasting it.
I like myself and I like my life
And I want to live it my way.

Chris Carter (12)
Blackthorn Middle School

HUNGRY

Aw, it's rumbling again,
Rumble, rumble.
I can feel pain.
It's rumbling and tumbling,
I could eat a sugar cane.

Sniff, sniff
I can smell food,
Burgers,
Chips,
And all that junk food.

Aw, it's rumbling again,
Rumble, rumble.
I can feel pain.
It's rumbling and tumbling,
I could eat a sugar cane.

Mmmmm!
Can you smell that?
Garlic bread,
And pizzas,
And loads of other meals.

Aw, it's rumbling again,
Rumble, rumble.
I can feel pain,
It's rumbling and tumbling,
I could eat a sugar cane.

Firyaal Ellahee (12)
Blackthorn Middle School

MY KIND OF WORLD

Every day I think to myself,
If I was powerful enough what would my world be like?
A world where there's no countries at war,
A world where a coloured person can go out at night,
A world where there is no crime,
That's my kind of world.

If I was powerful enough my world would be:
No children dying of poverty and these stupid wars,
No homeless people in pain on these streets,
No KKKs which ruin this world,
No people who abuse children for no reason,
That's my kind of world.

Krupa Unadkat (12)
Blackthorn Middle School

THE AWAKENING

The sun's mist creeps a gentle purple-blue,
The mountains have the fresh tint of green,
The sea shimmers and glistens,
With the sounds of dolphin's mating,
The sands have the soft-white glow, to touch, to feel.
The moors give a sweet scent of heather,
The fresh morning air is tinted with lavender,
New buds and leaves pierce through the soil,
Opening into blooms of colours, golds, oranges, reds and blues,
The awakening of the morning is here.

Ashley Galster (12)
Blackthorn Middle School

THE BASKETBALL GAME

Bouncing balls everywhere,
Aiming for the backboard.
Shooting, missed - what a shame!
Killer throws in the game,
Entering half-time,
The clock is ticking away.
Bounce pass, to the other team,
Attacking for the ball,
Little did they know,
Long-last, a goal!

Time's up oh dear they won,
Never mind!

Jayne Stanmore (13)
Blackthorn Middle School

THE NIGHT

Evening falls, night rises
With glistening stars shining brightly.
A breeze blows through the air,
Children hold their blankets tightly.
Lights go out one by one,
Darkness comes creeping.
Silence flows through the houses,
The moon above is lit.
Sleeping quietly,
Dreaming silently,
Hours pass,
As the night lasts.

Mandy Diep (12)
Blackthorn Middle School

WINTER ON THE STREETS

Snow, rain, sleet.
Constantly.
Slush turns to grey iron.
The bitter cold never ends.
Hostels full.
Subways, doorways, hard and cold.
In the eternal cold, death threatens.
Sleepless nights, endless days
Sleep, you may never wake up.

Tom Almond (12)
Blackthorn Middle School

MY DOG

My dog is a:
loud barker
cat chaser
hair moulter
flea catcher
human lover
stick catcher
ball player
piggy eater
furry body
tamed mate
fast as lightning.

Roxanne Bradford-Thom (11)
Blackthorn Middle School

ALL THROUGH THE YEAR

All the way through the year we have,
Leap years,
Lovely eggs come to children's joy.
The happiness of someone's birthday
Hallowe'en brings fright or joy.
Rings of people having fun.
Only one event of the year will bring the best of runs.
Ugly frights on Hallowe'en.
Gulping down the good food of normal days.
Happy will come all through the year.
Tall trees will breeze their way through windy days.
Hardy plants will keep nice and tidy.
Events will come all through the year.
Young lives being joyful.
Events are good as we go through the year.
And the joy it will bring for young, middle aged, elderly
Really nice people bring us the cool events we have
All through the year.

Samantha Nelligan (12)
Blackthorn Middle School

SILENCE

I sit alone in the dark, silence has come
He has escaped and kidnapped the sounds in the room.
There's not one single sound
I can't speak, I can't breathe.
He has locked all of the sounds in a bag.
Suddenly a breath escapes, silence has broken.
He runs off to a corner, waiting for the next time to strike.

Charlie Clark (11)
Blackthorn Middle School

FOOTBALL!

Fast feet kicking a ball
Only boys so they say
Or so they think
Trainers and boots kicking up the ball
Ball flying through the air
Arsenal, Man U, Chelsea
Late games
Last and final minutes
That's the whistle!
All over!

Louise Wright (12)
Blackthorn Middle School

SHARK

The shark prowls around the sea
King of all beasts, searching for food
He sees his prey, creeps up behind
Back fin propels through the water
He got his meal
He leaves.

Shane Wade (12)
Blackthorn Middle School

FISH

Scaly creature
Maggot eater
Shark's dinner
Rock beater
Spawning creature.

Tom Taylor (11)
Blackthorn Middle School

LOSING THE WORLD

Other countries fighting in fear,
Death lurking on the streets,
What is happening to this world?
Fighting, bombing in horror,
Why can't they just *stop!*
Families suffering the pain.
People dying in vain.
Children forced to leave their home.
Sitting here happily,
Other people are dying sadly,
We're lucky to live in a caring and loving country.

Rebecca Goodjohn (12)
Blackthorn Middle School

A LONELY RABBIT

I sit by my bowls every day,
Cramped by wooden walls,
I shiver in a cold, damp box,
Netting only to be seen,
My toes freeze,
My tongue dries in winter,
Never to be played with again.

A cold stale smell,
The toes of ice hang off my box,
The arms of warmth used to hold me,
Now I'm alone, all alone,
Love was lost, never seen again.

Lisa Greenwood (11)
Blackthorn Middle School

A GHOST

A ghost is white as snow
And it lives in my house.
It spooks me at night
When I'm in bed.
The ghost gives me goosebumps.
A nightmare seeker.
How long do I have to put up with it?
A ghost holds people hostage.
A street frightener.
It is the bone of death.
A floating blanket.
It is an emptiness.
And it makes the clock go
Bang?

Amie Kendall (13)
Blackthorn Middle School

BLUE WHALE

Slithers and swims around the sea
Sea lurker,
Enormous fish eater,
Sea splasher,
Human swallower,
Ocean ruler,
So call him what you like
But wait till you cross the sea.

Blayne Patmore (11)
Blackthorn Middle School

LONELY

I hate the way that I'm left out,
I hope they will appreciate me,
It isn't fair,
I want to cry.

It feels like they're laughing at me,
I don't know what to do.
They call me names and shout at me,
I don't like them at all.

Not a single friend,
They push and snarl at me,
I wish that it would end.
It feels like I'm punished,
For something I didn't do.

They hurt my feelings,
Tears are running down my face,
It's like a shooting star pricking me.

Sarah Williams (11)
Blackthorn Middle School

THEY'VE FORGOTTEN ME

The hay pinches like bees stinging,
Cobwebs follow me as if they were my shadows,
Empty cracked bowl, staring at me,
My water runs away to nothing,
Sunlight taken away,
Nothing to do,
Loneliness screams all the way down inside me,
My dreams feel alive,
My life feels dead.

Kerrie Cotman (12)
Blackthorn Middle School

WINTER

He whips up a storm
As he clambers along
Singing his wild and wintry song.

Trees turn all icy
With winter's cold touch.
Will the poor animals escape from his clutch?

Animals hiding
And animals playing.
Will he be going, or will he be staying?

He jumps over streams
And rolls down the hills.
With his warm coat, he never gets chills.

He and his friends
Jack Frost and Sam Ice
Come once a year, but sometimes come twice.

Winter snarls
With his cold, icy breath.
Will he just stop, or drive us to death?

Rebecca Stone (11)
Blackthorn Middle School

NEGLECTED

Locked up in a strawless cage.
Wondering if anyone loves me.
He bought me, he loved me,
And now he neglects me.
Suffering from hunger and thirst.
Lying, dying in a splintering cage.

Mark Duncan (11)
Blackthorn Middle School

GHOST POEM - BEWARE!

A ghost lives in a haunted house
Sometimes sits in a corner without a doubt
They're sometimes in your dreams at night
But they always give you a terrible fright
A ghost is cold breath
And sometimes has no head
A ghost is a transparent sheet
That has no feet
A nightmare seeker
A floorboard creaker
A ghost is a ghost.

Glen Pierre Roberts (13)
Blackthorn Middle School

GHOST POEM

A ghost is an invisible figure.
A ghost is a person frightener.
A ghost is a scary monster.
A ghost is a white spirit.
A ghost will follow you.
A ghost lives in an old house.
A ghost is going to get you
Oh no!
Ghost - run for your life!
Ah!

Paul Harry (12)
Blackthorn Middle School

TEACHER

Never call a teacher 'big head'
Never call a teacher 'smart bum'
Never call a teacher 'wrinkle face'
Never tell a teacher they can't race
Never call a teacher 'a coffee drinker'
Never call a teacher 'a fast eater'
Until it's home time!

Joanne Baxter (11)
Blackthorn Middle School

A CAT CALLED MINNIE

As she climbs onto the table,
Creeps behind the flowers,
Takes a piece of chicken,
Jumps down,
Runs to bed,
Gives chicken to missy,
Drinking mother's milk.

Victoria Jeffery (12)
Blackthorn Middle School

WHALE SONG

I watch
Helpless,
As a long, sharp pole
Zooms through my long scaly tail.
Wriggling and twisting for freedom
If only they could just understand the way I feel,
For after all, I harm no man.

David Roberts (11)
Blackthorn Middle School

THE WORLD TODAY

The world I live in,
Is now all full of microchips.
Phones, computers, televisions and more.
Way, way back then,
The only invention they had were ships.

The world I live in
Is full of different kinds of foods.
Hamburgers, chips, sweets and chocolate.
Way, way back then,
The only way they would eat was rude.

The world I live in,
Is full of crime.
Murderers, rapists, robbers and more.
Way, way, back then,
The only crime they had was in rhyme.

The world I live in,
Is fun for me and my friends.
I just hope that for my children's children
Unlike back then,
The sunshine will never end.

Kim Scriven (12)
Blackthorn Middle School

A GHOST

A ghost is an evil spirit.
A ghost is an invisible figure
A ghost is a moving shadow.
A ghost gives you a chill.
A ghost will follow you
A ghost is a floating cloud.
A ghost can walk through walls.
A ghost can be friendly.
A ghost can give you a sign
That is a ghost.

William Bell (12)
Blackthorn Middle School

LIFE

Life is worth living never waste it.
Life is precious to me,
Life is what makes me, *me,*
Life is something special,
I like my life just the way it is,
I will live my life as excitedly as I can,
I will have fun until my life ends,
Life.

Ben Glazier (11)
Blackthorn Middle School

GHOST

A ghost is an unearthly figure
As light as the wind
As gentle as a feather
A spine-chiller
A ghost is a spooky creature
A nightmare seeker
A transparent sheet
A ghost is like the devil
Waiting to kill your dreams
And fill your head with nightmares.

Paul Hancock (12)
Blackthorn Middle School

GHOSTS

A ghost is a bedroom seeker
A ghost is a spine-chiller
A ghost is a person frightener
A ghost is a gentle whisperer
A ghost is a floorboard creaker
A ghost is a garden seeker
A ghost is a floating white sheet.

Barbara Zydonik (12)
Blackthorn Middle School

HALLOWE'EN

On a scary night
When people wear spooky clothes
Witches ride their brooms.

Matthew Nicholls (11)
Daventry William Parker School

I LOVE FOOD

I is for ice-cream, cold and sweet.

L is for liquorice, black and sticky,
O ranges, olives, Opal Fruits and onions,
V is for vegetables, full of vitamins,
E ggs, scrambled, fried or poached.

F ruit, figs, fish and fresh bread,
O ysters are slippery and not for me,
O nly chocolate as thick as can be,
D o you love your food too?

Katherine Weller (11)
Daventry William Parker School

MY WORST HALLOWE'EN

Hey Mister Death don't make me smell your breath,
It'll knock me out cold and turn me bold.
Oy Mister Dracula won't scare me even if you get
Out your fangs I'll just shout 'He! He!'
I'll do you a deal if you don't make me squeal,
I won't call you manky instead I'll call you Franky.
Stay away zombie, I'll use my karate, hang on,
I know that voice, it's my mate Marlie.

Neil Murray (11)
Daventry William Parker School

THE OCEAN

Looking at the ocean
Seeing the deep, deep blue for miles,
A dolphin jumps in the distance,
In front of the hot red blazing sun,
Which spreads a red glow as the sun goes down,
The ocean smacks against the rocks and makes a huge roar,
Stronger and stronger the waves become
And then they attack the seabed,
Coral reefs become exposed,
Seaweed and pebbles are washed in,
Slowly it begins to get dark,
The water wrinkles in the wind,
Lying in my bed I can hear the wind dying down,
The waves have stopped tossing and turning and can't
Cause any more harm.

Natalie Bell (11)
Daventry William Parker School

CHRISTMAS DAY

Wake up, wake up, it's Christmas Day,
Open your presents and come and play,
'What did you get?' I got a bike,
'What did Lucy get?' She got a trike,
I got a PlayStation, come and see,
It's right near the Christmas tree.

Hollie Drinkwater (11)
Daventry William Parker School

THE ANGEL

She stood there like a white rose
With her golden hair flowing like the sea
One moment she was there
And then, the next she was gone.
She was the air that I breathed
The only one I trusted.
She had beautiful wings which were white as snow
She was as dainty as a swan
And yet had the power of hope
She lit a fire inside me
Which will never burn out
Now she is gone
But I will always remember the angel I met.

Lindsey Thompson (12)
Daventry William Parker School

HALLOWE'EN

H   Hallowe'en's the time of the year, when fright is in the town.
A   All people are alighting pumpkins to see them in the dark.
L   Looking up at the dark gloomy sky when owls come flying down.
L   Laughing witches casting evil spells that leave bright sparks.
O   Oooing around the shops looking for your breathtaking outfit.
W   Walking on your way home when you see a skeleton covered in
     blood marks.
E   Eating your sticky food from parties or trick or treating.
E   Eleven loud shouts and screams from a castle high on a hill.
N   Now is that enough to get you going?

Fae Unger (11)
Daventry William Parker School

HAMSTER

Hunky hamster,
As fast as can be,
Moving all about,
Staring at people,
Trying to get to sleep,
Eating all the food,
Running on his wheel.

Laura Barrell (12)
Daventry William Parker School

THE RABBIT

Really furry to the touch
And snuggled in the straw,
Biting a carrot,
Buried in the straw,
In his cosy little hutch,
The rabbit feels secure.

Gemma Bolderson (12)
Daventry William Parker School

THE TANKED TORTOISE

It sits staring,
Staring at nothing,
I watch as it feebly stumbles to its food
And starts chewing it.
Very alone, it stares again,
It's just a bored tanked tortoise

Alison Sargent (11)
Daventry William Parker School

POEM PLEASE MISS

Please Miss, I don't want to do PE,
I've hurt my head and grazed my knee.
Please Miss, please let me off,
Today I've got a dreadful cough.

Please Miss, I don't want to do PE,
My nails will chip and I've bruised my hip.
Please Miss, please let me off,
It will mess up my brand new hairdo.

Please Miss, I don't want to do PE,
My ankles started swelling up this afternoon.
Please Miss, please let me off,
They're starting to look like balloons.

Please Miss, I don't want to do PE,
I've used up all my excuses, can't you see?
Please Miss, you've got to let me off,
'Cause I've also forgotten my PE stuff!

Susan Joynson (13)
Daventry William Parker School

DAYDREAM

It's very dark, it's twelve at night,
I'm walking in the park.
The wind is blowing, something's glowing,
It's just something in the dark.
It's not, it's real, it's closer now,
This thing that's in the dark,
A ghost, a spirit, a witch or maybe two,
No I must be dreaming, it's only ten-past two.

Siann Grant (11)
Daventry William Parker School

A MOONLIT WALK

As I walk along the warm, sandy beach, the moon
Shines out, piercing the darkness of the sky.
The cool, refreshing water of the sea, laps against my feet.
Boats silently float along the decks of the harbour
Palm trees violently rustle in the wind.
Light from the lighthouse shines out for miles,
Guiding whoever comes near.
Seagulls swoop down to catch their midnight feast,
A fish or two at least.
Here I am, all alone.
The humid air closing in around me,
As I sit and watch the night turn to dusk.

Helen Trueman (13)
Daventry William Parker School

RED IS MY FAVOURITE

Red is the colour of roses,
Red is the colour of love,
Red is the colour of hearts,
Red is the colour of my heart,
Red is the colour of my carpet,
Red is the colour of life,
Red is the colour of royal,
Red is the colour of my pen,
Red is the colour of my compass,
Red is the colour of the world.

Jenny Cooper (11)
Daventry William Parker School

IN THE PARK

On one cold Monday night,
In the park.
As a storm grew
It blew swings to their sides
As the storm grew bigger and bigger.

On one hot and sunny Tuesday morning
A bee hovered by my side
As the sun shone all day long
In the park.

On Wednesday in the park
The skies grew darker by the minute
Letting rain and hail fall down like bombs
As lightning pierced its way down from the sky.

On one windy Thursday night in the park
Gales whipped the trees to their sides,
Then there was a big bang of thunder
As the stormy night had just begun.

On one misty Friday morning in the park
It started to rain . . .
But then the sun came out
Then it formed a rainbow.

Rachael Hopper (12)
Daventry William Parker School

THE BRILLIANCE OF TELEVISION

Television is the best,
I couldn't live a day without it,
I praise the person who made it,
It's the best invention ever.

I can just sit there all day,
Cuddling up in a nice warm chair,
Not having to move a muscle,
Apart from changing the channel.

The programmes are just getting better and better,
Friends, Eastenders, Simpsons and millions more,
What's even better is Sky and Digital,
The choices are unlimited.

Sophie Pritchard (12)
Daventry William Parker School

CHRISTMAS

C ards through the door on Christmas Day,
H appy people coming to stay,
R ibbon on a wreath which hangs upon the door,
I ce which settles upon the floor,
S tocking hung beside my bed,
T insel which glistens a powerful red,
M agnificent presents under the tree,
A ll night I wonder which present's for me,
S anta's coming, yippee!

Melissa Mudge (12)
Daventry William Parker School

SAUSAGES

Sausages are so great,
When they are for tea, I'm never late,
Sizzling in a pan, or sitting on a plate,
Hot or cold, I just can't wait.

Sausages are fun,
Perched on a stick, or tucked in a bun,
On their own or however they come,
I can never resist having some.

Sausages are tasty
Pork or beef, with chips or pastry
Thick or thin, straight or curly
With mash, batter or curly whirly.

Sausages are great,
When they are for tea I'm never late,
If I don't get them, I'm sure to create
So Mum . . . just fill my plate!

Simon Hudson (12)
Daventry William Parker School

THE SUNSET

Orange sun
Half you can see
Half you can't
With a nice cool breeze
It gets darker and darker
As the night goes on.
Suddenly it's pitch-black,
No light, no sun,
No sunset.

Samantha Beames (13)
Daventry William Parker School

SNOWBALL FIGHTS

Snowball fights are a lot of fun,
Whether the battle's lost or won.

Start off with four teams of three,
Build a base,
Get a snowball in your face,
The opposition shouting, we'll kill you if you don't flee.

They take over your base,
You say 'We have to get it back,'
And 'Quick move Jack'
Too late cos he got a snowball in his face.

Snowball fights are a lot of fun,
Whether the battle's lost or won.

We build a snow wall to protect all of us
And we ally with a team,
So that all six of our faces glowed with a beam,
Snowball thrown at a passing bus.

Getting late and getting cold,
I'm wet but not giving up,
Tom to defend his base, built a wicket,
Get in now I got told.

Snowball fights are a lot of fun,
Whether the battle's lost or won.

Tim Storrow (12)
Daventry William Parker School

SNOW AND JACK FROST

Here comes snow,
Very slow.
One by one they came,
Against the window frame.
I just saw Jack Frost,
I thought he was lost.
I ran out to play,
And said, 'Hey, hey, hey.'
Then he trembled with fright,
As the sun started to bright,
For his life he feared
As he disappeared.

Peter J Genockey (11)
Daventry William Parker School

HALLOWE'EN

H aunted houses on Hallowe'en,
A ll we do is make you scream,
L ots of frights,
L ots of fun,
O nly witches need to come,
W itches brew and poison too,
E ntertainment for me and you,
E very witch is out to play,
N ight-time horror for only one day.

Andrea Griffin (11)
Daventry William Parker School

WHY?

Why do we have homework?
Why do we have school?
Why does it seem like teachers rule?

Why are there big kids to push us around?
Why can't we make the tiniest sound?

Why is there school uniform?
Why is everything precise?
Why are some teachers nasty and other's nice?

Why do we do maths and science and history?
To me, all this is such a mystery.

I don't know the answers - Do you?

Gemma Harris (11)
Daventry William Parker School

FIRE DRAGON

I know something you don't know,
A fire dragon lives down the road.
He lives in a cave all down and low,
Because he ran out of toads,
His favourite food.
He is friendly to me
'Cause I totally agree,
With the colours of his fire.
I want to inspire,
Other kids.

Lara Harvey
Daventry William Parker School

FRIENDS

What is a friend?
Someone caring,
Helpful and thoughtful?
Someone pleasant,
Kind and faithful?

What does a friend look like?
Someone with freckles,
Bunches and big teeth?
Someone blonde,
Pale skinned and pretty?

What does a friend do?
Do they help you with your homework?
Look after you and support you?
Do they cheer for you?
Play with you and care for you?

I don't know, but I wish I had some.

Rebecca Hibberd (11)
Daventry William Parker School

THE DOLPHIN SHOW

The dolphin show is very cruel
Because they keep them in a pool.
They make them jump through lots of hoops
They even make them balance balls.
They make them do a winding twist,
So it looks good as they catch the fish.
I think they should let all the dolphins free
So they can live in the wide open sea.

Chrystal Marie Sharp (12)
Daventry William Parker School

MY PET DOG BECKY

My pet dog named Becky is the cutest and cuddliest thing,
The unknown border collie with Egyptian eyes,
Cute, well behaved, well trained, the best loveable friend ever,
Nine years old and 63 in dog years and still not tired
                          or showing any important signs.
The only dog I have seen totally ball crazy and excited
                          when we say *walkies.*
The triangle like ears shoot up like a rocket when she hears *walkies.*
Get the lead and take her out for a walk and when you come
Back you will be her best friend. A few months later, it's time for
A bath, she sprints (runs) for her life behind the settee.
She will come to you if you tell her to.
When she's in the bath she will try and jump out again.
That's my poem about my pet dog Becky.

Damien Turland (11)
Daventry William Parker School

MY MUM AND DAD

My dad is a rally technician,
He doesn't like fishing.
He flies to lots of countries
And doesn't mind
Because he knows he has a good time.
My mum likes doing the garden
So everything is neat
And then she gets in a hot bath
To soak her feet,
My mum and dad
Make me glad.

Alyson Batty (12)
Daventry William Parker School

THE BEST SPORT

Football: Football's a sport that everyone knows
The game ends when the final whistle blows.
One famous player has the name of Paul Scholes,
The aim of the game is to score the most goals.

Basketball: Basketball's a sport that has two teams,
The nets are held up by metal beams,
They pass the ball and bounce it around,
It's a sport that brings a big crowd.

Golf: Golf's a sport where you have a small ball,
It's a calm sport so there's no time at all,
They use metal sticks with a lump on the end,
The green may be sloped so the ball path may bend.

Rugby: Rugby's a game where you wear a gum shield,
You play on grass known as a field,
It's a famous game, been around for years,
When you lose a big game there might be tears.

But speedway's the best and will be for years.

Matthew Nixon (11)
Daventry William Parker School

MY HAMSTER HARRY

Harry is a hamster,
Small and sweet.
He has soft round ears
And tiny pink feet.
He is busy all night
Then sleeps soundly all day,
Curled up tight in his nest of hay.

Ashleigh Englert (11)
Daventry William Parker School

MILLENNIUM BUG

It's in the papers,
It's on the news,
It's on the radio,
It's everywhere!

Millennium Bug!

Is it big?
Is it small?
Will it chase me?
Why is it after me?
Will it eat me?
Will I defeat it?
When is it coming?
Is it an ant?
Is it a bee?

What is it?

I don't know.

I don't know much, that makes me scared,
But let's just hide until . . .
Whenever it comes,
I don't know!

Siobhain Larkin (13)
Daventry William Parker School

THE EXAM

On that table
In that chair
Pen and paper, there they glare.

One clock ticking,
Someone else tapping,
One person coughing,
One chair squeaking.

Pen at the ready,
Time to begin,
No more talking.

The hall goes silent
Pens move quickly
10 minutes remain
Have all the questions been answered?

Hayley Anne Page (12)
Daventry William Parker School

AT A FOOTBALL GAME

Running down the wing,
Listening to the crowd sing,
Scoring goals by the minute,
As fast as a speeding bullet.
Dribbling like a baby,
Pass it back to Taibi
Who stops all the shots
That come from Steve Potts.

Danny Beech (13)
Daventry William Parker School

MILLENNIUM HOPES AND DREAMS

I have a dream,
That someday in the future,
Life will be full of happiness,
With no fears or problems.

No death, no pain,
No killing without reason,
Hurting families, breaking hearts,
Life, it is really hard.

Racism, why oh why?
They're only normal people,
We should just let them be,
Give them all a chance.

Poverty, no food or clothes,
Glad for love and care,
Everyone could do their bit,
They really need our help.

Cancer, how terrible,
I wish there was a cure,
Therapy is long and painful,
Life can be so cruel.

Without these things,
Life would be peaceful and calm,
I know they won't ever disappear,
But I have a dream.

Rachel Finch (13)
Daventry William Parker School

EARLY MORNING AT THE BEACH

As I walk along the seashore,
Feeling the damp sand beneath my feet
And the cool breeze against my face
I slowly turn and look out to sea
It seems so calm.
The only sound is the rippling of the
Waves on the shore
As they hit the seashore they seem
To melt beneath the sand
I move closer
The sea touches my feet
It is so cold
It feels like ice.
Just appearing over the horizon is a
Big ball of fire
Gradually it rises into the sky
Bringing a new day
The sea glistens beneath its glow.
I can hear the sound of seagulls
As they fly out for breakfast
Heading for the fishing boats which
Are returning home.

Charlene Murfin (12)
Daventry William Parker School

THE OLD MAN

There is this old man down my street,
Who only goes out at night.
He walks around the town,
Again and again,
Constantly walking.

As the sun rises
He rushes back home,
During the day
He sits on a chair, looking into space,
Rocking back and forth.

He must be lonely,
Sitting there, all day,
His family have forgot about him.
I might go to see him
To make him feel alive again.

I went around his house yesterday,
He's very nice.
We talked about when he was in the Navy.
A once very important captain of a ship,
Forgotten,
Forgotten forever.

Robert Horne (13)
Daventry William Parker School

WAR

Why do people declare war?
There must be a reason,
Why do people shoot and fight?
Will we ever make them see light?
Why do people bomb places
And create such sad looks on people's faces?
Why do people have to make agreements
To stop all the war?
And why is peace so hard to find?
Why do innocent people have to die?
And why do peace leaders have to lie?
How can we stop this terrible thing?
To stay at home
And pray to God it will go away.
Why is it that we can't just stop . . .
All the fighting?
All the shooting?
All the terrorism?
Why?
Because it's war.

Nicky Willies (12)
Daventry William Parker School

FISHING

I want to go fishing on the creak
I want to see the ripples on the water upon the lake.

When the sun glistens on the water,
The lake looks like the sky.
Silvery slippery scales of the wriggling
Fish glint in the sun.

I catch a fish
Hurrah! I say
But its eyes stare at me
Its gills flapping widely gasping
For air pleading.

So I let it go
Back in the lake.

Luke Stephenson (11)
Daventry William Parker School

BUILDINGS

Buildings are a great surprise
Everyone's a different size,
Offices
Grow
Long
And
High
Tall
Enough
To
Touch
The
Sky,
Houses seem more like a box,
Made with glue and building blocks,
Every time you look you see,
Buildings shaped quite differently.

Daniel Cowley (12)
Daventry William Parker School

MY GRAN

The games we played, the fun we had,
When with you I never was sad.
Spotting birds was always your hobby,
A sparrow, a hawk, a redbreast robin.
Never sad, glum or angry,
Just the sight of you made everyone happy.

The terrible news made everyone cry,
In disbelief that you were to die.
I got a warm feeling from your loving touch,
So many people will miss you so much.
And so the cancer took its toll,
It killed your body but not your soul.

Chris Moon (12)
Daventry William Parker School

AUTUMN

Crispy, blue skies
Nights drawing in,
Golden falling leaves,
Turning cold and frosty
Hats and gloves,
Bare trees
Bed of golden leaves,
Hallowe'en and Bonfire Night.
Grass stops growing
Migrating birds
Hibernating animals
Autumn.

Katie Hancox (12)
Daventry William Parker School

FIRE

Fire!
Breezing through a dark forest
Charging like an army heading to war.
It sweeps
Disappears into a log.
As the log starts to burn,
It rolls down a hill
To a river
Like a person calling their pet to come to them
The log jumps and falls
Into a raging torrent of water
It is like the log sacrificed itself
To save the forest,
The fire is gone.

Gary Hutt (11)
Daventry William Parker School

NIGHTMARE

N ight has come, the shadows appear,
I   snuggle down in my bed, tremble with fear,
G rasping my pillows, I try to sleep,
H earing noises, I had to leap,
T he light was near, I switched it on,
M y heart was pumping, the fear had gone,
A s I switched the light off and snuggled back down,
R aging thoughts raced through my mind as I frowned,
E ventually, I got some sleep by counting one
                        hundred and twenty sheep.

Stephanie Cox (13)
Daventry William Parker School

FOOTBALL CRAZY

I'm football crazy,
I'm football mad,
I follow Birmingham City
Just like my old dad.

I like going to watch the matches,
The prices are quite insane,
But it doesn't stop me coming back,
Time and time again.

I love it in the terraces,
The brilliant atmosphere,
The waving of scarves and banners,
The deafening roars and cheers.

My favourite player is Peter Ndlovu
You should see him run down the wing,
His boots dance round the players,
Then the crowd start to sing.

The crowd stamp their feet,
Because they want more,
'Go on Birmingham! Go on and score!

The final whistle goes,
The game has come to an end
Birmingham were rather poor,
Only managing a 1-1 draw.

Daniel Lee (13)
Daventry William Parker School

PARENTS! THE GOOD - THE BAD

There are times when we think that our parents are the best,
They can be your closest friends.
But parents change all the time
And that's when the friendship ends!

Take me for example, I love Mum and Dad,
They do so much for me.
But then in return they set impossible tasks,
They may as well be the enemy!

They shop around and buy all the trendiest clothes,
They cheer in every football match I play.
When I do well in school they puff up with pride,
They claim I brighten up their day!

But every so often a dark day comes,
There are always some days which go wrong.
Our views may clash, I may lash out
And I feel that I don't belong!

I admit those times are quite horrible,
They always hurt so much.
But by far there are more good days than bad,
There's no competition as such!

My mum and dad no matter what,
We'll always stick together,
They'll always be there whenever I need them
And I know I'll love them . . . forever!

Rakesh Patel (13)
Daventry William Parker School

SMILE

You grit your teeth and widen your eyes,
Pull your cheeks high, give a look of surprise.
You know when you have done this, your problem
Will fade maybe even stay like this, they will go away.

You greet a friend with a smile
It brightens their day,
A smile is the best way of communication,
Transforming a face, each has a story,
Everyone can smile, everyone needs to once in a while.
Don't hold back, just grit your teeth,
Widen your eyes and give your best look of surprise.

Every morning when you rise, put a smile on your face,
Brave the day,
Every time you smile a problem may go away.
So just remember when you're in a crisis,
Smile and smile away!

Kelly Courtney (13)
Daventry William Parker School

BASKETBALL

Basketball is really cool
And the players are extremely tall.
You've gotta be a really fast runner
And a fantastic shunner.

Michael Jordan is my hero
He could even beat Ray Mystreo.
He has done so many slam dunks
He could go without training for a month.

David Best (11)
Daventry William Parker School

GHOST BEACH

It was cold,
Silent,
Foggy even,
You could hear children,
Who cried,
Help, help, help me,
They seem as real as you
And me,
They were as pale as the sea.

As the children disappeared a
Pier appeared.
It was strange,
The pier was the same colour,
As pale as the children
It was as if I was on
Ghost beach.

Amy Majda (12)
Daventry William Parker School

DOLPHIN WORLD

Teeth as soft as a newborn puppy,
Nose as blunt as a fingertip,
Skin as smooth as silk,
Gentle as the night.
Fins like rubber just fingering the top of the sea,
Friendly, calm, lovely, jumpy and
Proud of its place in the animal world.

Laura Hargraves (11)
Daventry William Parker School

THE SPECIAL SALE

On Hallowe'en all the witches in the world rush down to the mall,
Because on this special night,
In this special town,
In this special world,
All the witches love the special sale.

And in this special sale you can buy special things:

Three pence of spiders - witches need them lots, for spells of every kind,
Cut price worms - same price just cut in half,
Reduced rats - just on a diet of nothing,
Bargain bats - they fly all over the place.

So that's why this year on this special night,
In this special town,
In this special world,
The whole special thing was off.

Amanda Hoyle (12)
Daventry William Parker School

AUTUMN

As the brownish leaves
Slowly descended from the treetops,
The cool autumn breeze filled the air
Blowing the falling leaves to distant places.

The trees shaking as the wind blows
Making the leaves look like a raging storm,
Leaves were everywhere,
As neatly raked piles flew like snow.

David Renard (13)
Daventry William Parker School

WHAT AM I?

What am I?
That is the question
I'm cute and furry
And friendly you know.

My coat can be short or long
But sometimes it can pong
It can be scruffy or tidy
I sometimes play hidy.

The colours can vary
From white through to brown
Ginger and brown are quite common
But black and grey are quite rare.

I rustle my bed
And fill my pouch
I gnaw on wood to file my teeth
I sleep through the day and eat at night.

My diet is varied
I really don't mind
I like lots of veggies
But no teddies.

My tail is short and stubby
My belly can be quite tubby
And my legs are very stubby
Have you guessed what I am?

Claire Hutchinson (11)
Daventry William Parker School

MY HAMSTER DOODLES

My hamster Doodles has longish hair,
When I stroke him he doesn't care,
He runs in his ball out the door, into the hall
And then he sits down and looks really cool.
He likes eating sweetcorn he gives it a gnaw,
But when he's finished, he chucks it on the floor,
He likes climbing up the bars,
He hates the sound of noisy cars.

He climbs so high like an acrobat,
He hates to see a nasty cat,
He picks about at his food,
Really he is a cool dude,
But now he's deceased and passed away,
In his cage, there's only straw and hay.

Tim Saunders (12)
Daventry William Parker School

THERE IS AN ALIEN IN MY HOUSE

There is an alien in my house
His name is Sid
He has an interest in my mouse
And the dustbin lid.

He made front page on the Daventry Express
To which scientists took a great interest
Lots of things went on from there
But Sid didn't care.

I wish I could put him in a big suitcase
And send him back to outer space.

Hayley Croft (11)
Daventry William Parker School

CHANGES

The leaves are turning brown and gold,
Squirrel storing nuts before the cold
Memories of a long hot summer day
Seems now to be an age away.

Good feelings now of times ahead,
Of freezing nights snug in bed
Seasonal thoughts around the tree
Presents handed for you and me.

And now millennium is here
Rejoicing of the brand new year
Spring will very soon be seen
With the leaves again turning green.

Tom Parratt (11)
Daventry William Parker School

A WORLD OF AUTUMN

The frost is twinkling upon the grass,
as I stroll along,
I see the leaves have changed in colour,
and will soon be falling down.

Then suddenly I see the moon,
appear from behind a frost-bitten house,
so bright with a distinctive twinkle,
as it glides through the azure sky.

Now finally my walking stops,
along with the crunch of the frosty grass,
and as I enter the light and warmth,
a world of autumn is left behind . . .

David Guest (12)
Daventry William Parker School

UNTITLED

Leaves are falling,
dropping like flies,
floating silhouettes against
autumn skies.

The trees are shedding their
golden coat.
The leaves don't fall
just gently float.

Leaves are falling,
dropping like flies,
floating silhouettes against
autumn skies.

Beth Milburn (12)
Daventry William Parker School

AUTUMN CHANGES

Brown leaves come,
Green ones gone.
These littered paths,
I walk upon.

The shadow of a tree,
Looking like Jack Frost.
This vicinity is desolated,
The village lost.

So all the leaves have fallen,
Jack Frost has come and gone.
And now I'm waiting patiently,
For the summer sun.

Matthew Hemmington (13)
Daventry William Parker School

AUTUMN

I pull my coat tighter,
As the frost settles on the grass,
The fallen leaves have made a path,
For me to walk along.

The stars in the sky,
Twinkle like jewels,
The bright and shiny moon,
Peers up over the hills.

The forest animals,
Scurry around,
Looking for food,
Then back to their nests they go.

I get home and go to bed,
My warm, warm bed,
And dream,
Dream about the wonders of autumn . . .

Stuart Clarke (12)
Daventry William Parker School

MONSTERS

Monsters are scary,
All big and hairy.
Their teeth are all sharp,
Like tips of a dart.
Some are big and bumpy,
Others are small and dumpy.

Louise Piper (11)
Daventry William Parker School

MY MATE LAURA

My mate Laura is really cool,
But can sometimes act like a bit of a fool.
She likes to be as loud as she can,
She's the kind of person who'll scare your nan.
She's loveable but kind of mad,
She's always drooling over a lad.
She's a really good friend,
And I'm glad she's mine,
We've known each other for ages and we get on fine.
Now I've finished my poem about Laura,
If you didn't like it I'm sorry I bored ya!

Victoria Thompson (13)
Daventry William Parker School

FOUR SEASONS

In the winter snowmen are made,
Then overnight fresh snow is laid.
In the spring the sun is oh so bright,
At 9pm it's still quite light.
In the summer it's very hot,
Oh look at all the sunburn I've got.
In the autumn the leaves go brown,
Then they all fall down.
All that's left is Christmastime,
When everything goes fine.

Tim Smith (13)
Daventry William Parker School

SNOWFLAKES

Snowflakes are unusual creatures,
Their magical presence,
Their intricate features.

Their elegant poise,
And tranquil flight.
They're enchanting, mystic,
A beautiful sight.

Their angel-like image,
Unique in every way.
Their drifting movements
Sailing through the day.

Their pristine appearance,
So pure and white.
Their dainty manner,
And illuminating light.

Their dazzling charm,
Displayed in the sky like stars.
Their entrancing motions,
As they wander far.

Their journey will soon
Come to an end.
The snowflakes will settle
On the white blanket they send.

Rachel Attenburrow (14)
Daventry William Parker School

DISASTROUS DAVID

One day Disastrous David
got bored with staying inside,
so he went off down the street,
in search of interesting things to find.

He hadn't gone very far at all
when he came across a banana skin,
but by the time he realised it was there,
he'd gone flying and cut open his chin.

In fact by the time he reached the town,
he'd had more than his fair share of fun.
He'd been scratched by a cat,
got stuck in a gate,
and was very lucky not to have drowned.

He carried on till he reached the zoo,
but this trip was to be cut short.
An unfortunate incident with some angry piranhas,
meant that he left with less fingers than he ought.

But David being the determined person he is,
decided to learn how to ski,
but that had to end after only a few minutes,
after he collided head on with a tree.

So skiing forgotten he turned to football,
and decided to play as goalkeeper,
but he was knocked unconscious
not long into the game
after he mistakenly headbutted the bar.

But he *had* to find something to do
where in some way he wouldn't get hurt,
so he decided to go camping in the wilderness,
but got eaten by a bear named Bert!

Well Disastrous David's life came to an end,
but he did have an eventful life,
The only problem seemed to be,
it was full of pain, and agony and strife.

Mark Odell (14)
Daventry William Parker School

MOONLIGHT NIGHT

Moonlight guides our paths
with the help of the stars.
Dew on the grass, the smell of fresh air.
We're all playing without a care.
It's cold and eerie
but people are cheery.
Trees are whispering, birds are chirpy,
we're all on a high all happy and quirky.
Light has faded the sky has turned dark grey
everyone is trying to have their say.
The wind is getting up, the trees are
turning into funny shapes.
Ghosts are waiting in their white capes.
The light has totally gone, the atmosphere is dead
Mums are calling to tuck their children into bed.
We all depart the ghosts are ready
I walk up the hill really steady
I'm frightened of things that lie ahead
I just wanted to get into bed.
I'm nearly there into some light
I've made it out of this eerie night.

Alison Crockford (14)
Daventry William Parker School

THE ARGUMENT

'Hey you, get off that's mine!'
'No it's not, I told you last time.'
'Give me that back, I hate you.'
'That's not fair, I hate you too.'
'I want it back, I want it now.'
'No, that's mine. Stop this row!'
'No I won't, I want my top.'
'That top is mine and I won't stop.'
'Shut your face and give that me!'
'That is mine, I don't give in easily.'
Three hours later the top tore,
Now the argument's worse than before.

Heather Owen (13)
Daventry William Parker School

SHEEP

I often go wandering far and near,
just to see a little dear.
Its coat is so fluffy and really white
although it's heavy, it looks so light.

They skip through meadows bright and green,
if you see one you'll know what I mean.
Go on have a look, just one peep,
you'll love them like I do those adorable *sheep!*

Laura Reynolds (14)
Daventry William Parker School

BAKE A SCHOOL

Take,
        a classroom gigantic or small
decorated with pictures full of many colours.

Add,
        a spoonful of teachers small and tall
writing on the blackboard with bright-coloured chalk.

Sprinkle,
        some books fascinating or boring
into a large, open spacious library.

Spread,
        a long narrow corridor with albums
full of photos of the school.

Melt,
        noisy computers followed by their
ancestors the rattling printers.

Whisk,
        the staffroom full of comforting teachers
while drinking their coffee.

Then finally cover with friendly people to
reveal William Parker School.

Sunita Sorroy (12)
Daventry William Parker School

I HAD A DREAM

I had a dream,
I met the Queen.
She had a monster,
Who's name was Donster.
He wore a hat,
He was quite fat.
He lived in muck,
And drove a truck.
he had long hair,
Only ate bear.
He had one brother,
They hated one another.
His name was Bob,
Bob was a slob,
And had no job.
Donster's mate was a mouse,
Who lived in a house.
One day he died,
Donster cried.
He cried so much,
He washed away the muck.
But when Donster died,
No one cried,
Even Bob
Who had no job.
he just cheered,
And stroked his beard.
When I woke up,
I remembered the muck.
I remembered Donster,
Who was a monster.

I told my dad,
Who was also sad
As he knew Donster,
That nice old monster.

Ben Killeen (12)
Daventry William Parker School

THE DOG NEXT DOOR

The dog next door keeps me
awake all night.
It keeps me awake until
the morning becomes light.

Dog next door
please stop barking
is there something wrong?
Have you been shut away for too long?

Dog next door,
I'll bribe you with a bone.
If you don't accept this,
I'll call your owner on the phone.

Finally, the dog next door
went all quiet.
I miss that little dog now
he doesn't seem to make a riot.

Mary Ahmadi (13)
Daventry William Parker School

PARENTS

Parents are always there to help
and to love you and to care.
I don't know where I'd be without them
I know that they're always there.

You may just think they chatter on
but listen to what they say.
They always say what you need to hear
and help you on your way.

There may be times you scream and shout
and not get on at all.
They keep on moaning and get you bored
and make you look a fool!

But deep down inside, you know you love them
and they love you too, you'll see
but sometimes you think you're only there
just to make the tea!

Rachael Maplethorpe (14)
Daventry William Parker School

THE MONSTER IN THE RIVER

There's something in the river

M y body starts to shiver
O ver the river
N ight is drawing in
S keleton in the bin
T errible monster's rising
E verything is scary
R un because there's something hairy.

Nathan Wheeler (12)
Daventry William Parker School

THE BULLIES

They're coming.
You know what they're after.
They're after your money, your books,
and most of all . . . *you!*

'Give us your money!
Hand us your books!'
And then they go to the other side of the
playground and copy your answers.

You get back in the classroom,
no book, no bag.
The teacher won't believe you,
and keeps you in after school.
The bullies sitting at their desks.
Laughing, sniggering.

Helen Ward (11)
Daventry William Parker School

PEOPLE

Tall and short, fat and thin
it makes no difference how they are within.
Eyes and ears, mouth and nose,
a big long chin and wonky toes.
Hair maybe curly, maybe straight,
it makes no difference to your mate.
Evil, wicked, cruel or kind,
a nicer side of them you may find.
No matter what they say or do
they're a person just like you.

Michelle Burdon (13)
Daventry William Parker School

NOSES

Big noses, small noses,
You see them all around,
Hairy noses, spotty noses,
On people's face they can be found.

Squeezey noses, hard noses,
Not easy to blow,
Pointy noses, long noses
When they go red they can glow.

Lumpy noses, straight noses,
Which one is mine,
Roman noses, turned up noses,
Mine looks quite fine.

I'm glad I like my nose,
I think it's really cool,
It's not big or squeezy
So I don't look like a fool!

Ben Murrell (13)
Daventry William Parker School

A GIRL IN MY CLASS

There's a girl in my class, with lovely ginger hair.
She will not go out with me. I think it's not fair.

I like her face, every little bit and
I like her because she's fit.
She says she hates me, I know it's a lie
but when she says it, I want to cry.

She's warm and friendly, she's really kind
every minute she's in my mind.

Ben Smith (12)
Daventry William Parker School

SCHOOL MORNINGS

I can't get up in the morning,
Because I'm lying in bed snoring,
The birds are singing,
My alarm bell is ringing,
And another school day is dawning.

Breakfast is ready and waiting for me,
Toast and jam and a nice cup of tea.
I can hear Mum calling me down,
But I'm lying in bed being a clown.

I must get up and get myself dressed,
Wash my hair and look my best.
I'm walking to school with my best mate,
So I'd better get a move on,
Or I'm going to be late.

Daniel Webb (12)
Daventry William Parker School

DOLPHINS

I go to a place where dolphins swim below the deep, blue sea
I see their shiny, silky fins as they skim through the sea in
twos and threes.

I sit there for hours just sitting there watching them skimming,
skimming through the water.

I hear them calling for their mates and crying for them too.
The sound is nice when I stroke their noses, they're soft and
smooth too.

Leanne Duffy (12)
Daventry William Parker School

SUNFLOWERS

A dark green bud
opening to its new world.
Soon the golden petals
will be uncurled.

Here's our sunflower
swaying in the delicate breeze.
It will soon be as tall
as all of the trees.

Lovely bold petals
clear and bright.
It's a fantastic, dazzling
and beautiful sight.

All of the seeds
are small and striped.
All of the birds wait
until they are ripe.

Slowly the flower leaves
from the place go all
dry and wrinkly and
disowns its face.

Dead on the ground
this flower will lay.
It's life is now over
it is no longer gay.

Connie Cook (11)
Daventry William Parker School

CROSS COUNTRY

Running, running
as fast as you can go!
You're nearly at the finish line
but you're really going slow!

You think your legs are dead
and your face is going red!
You're dying for a stop
and you really want to drop!

At last you're at the finish line,
your body all aglow.
Your feet are hot and sticky
but now, not wanting to slow.

Hollie Gardner (11)
Daventry William Parker School

WHO AM I?

I suck people's blood
I crawl around the mud
I have fangs that sting
I leave a slight sting
I am dressed in black
I like to attack
Blood is the thing I desire
But am I a vampire?
No! I'm a blood sucking tick!

Matthew Pettit (13)
Daventry William Parker School

SNOW LEOPARD

Snow leopard keeping low
In the mist of the snow.

Snow leopard hunting hare
With sharp claws ripping it bare.

Snow leopard not bare
But they are very rare.

Paul Krampf (11)
Daventry William Parker School

THE GRIMER

G rimer, look out, it's behind ya.
R oar! Watch out, I think it's behind the door.
I look under the bed, I see its head.
M ust watch out Grimer's about
E ating my toes, smelling with its nose
R ight under my bed it's going for my head.

James Shackleford (12)
Daventry William Parker School

A FIELD OF DAFFODILS

In the fields and far away
The daffodils bloom to come out and play
If you see them blowing around
Just wait and watch for them to settle down.

Daniel Drury (12)
Latimer Community Arts College

THE FOOTBALLER

The winger skilful and powerful,
His name is Leigh McFall
He's not slow but fast
The defender soon will be past.

The shout is, 'One-two!'
But from who?
Was it Jim, or
Was it Tim?

The run does not stop,
Because the player's on top;
A player approaches,
With support from his coaches.

That's still not a worry,
He's beaten in a flurry.
Coming in from the wing,
Yes! The ball has gone in.

A celebration is in need,
And celebrate he does indeed.
A shot from forty yards out,
Goal of the month without a doubt.

The final whistle is blown,
The player's name is quickly known.
The score is two-one,
And Holting Lions have won.

Jonathon Mark Burrows (12)
Latimer Community Arts College

IT WAS SITTING THERE

It was sitting there.
In the middle of the room,
In a large bucket.

I felt like I was going to faint.

My heart was pounding
Really fast.
I went up to it.

One of my friends said,
'You're not going to do it.'
I wanted to prove her wrong,
So I put my hand in.

I let the crab crawl up my arm
To my elbow.

When it got there my friends started counting.
My legs were shaking,
My heart was beating
Really fast.

I was going to make it, 'Fifty, sixty, seventy, one hundred.'
Halfway!

I was going to collapse,
Then -
Twenty more seconds to go.
I knew I was going to do it.

Ten, five, zero.

I had done it. I collapsed
On the floor.
A sense of relief went through my body.

It's over.

Stacey Sutton (12)
Latimer Community Arts College

TULIPS

A tulip standing straight and tall
Tower over creatures so very, very small
Sheltered from the rain,
And the howling wind and deathly pain of earth.

Throwing arms of greeny leaves
Hoping to attract the humming bees.
Sitting in the shade watching the world go by.
Not knowing that he soon will die.

The summer after, he is old
His edges are wilting.
Soon after he disappeared under protective hedges
The tulip is gone forever and longer
But in its place a sapling much stronger.

William Duggan (12)
Latimer Community Arts College

KALEIDOSCOPE

Round and round
Up and down
Things flow into memory
Forgotten birthdays
Lost Christmases
Big daisies
Small sunflowers
Dogs walking humans
Grass in the sky
And pigs fly
These things are back to front
Am I dreaming?
My world swirls
I swim on land
I walk on the sea
I eat with my feet rather than my hands
Then suddenly I wake up
Everything is normal rather than a kaleidoscope.

Katherine Hallen (12)
Latimer Community Arts College

MY SUNFLOWER POEM!

A shimmering sunflower
Shining in the sun
Sparkling with the stars
Waving in the breeze.

It stands alone
Long and slender
Taking in the summer sunshine
Standing amongst its many friends.

Joanne Fox (12)
Latimer Community Arts College

THE ROSE

As the red, red rose blows in the wind.
Its petals fall like raindrops of silk.
The rose it stands so bright and tall, that anything
next to it looks so small.
The rose, its petals so deep with red.
It is like a silky thread.
The rose is pretty, the rose is tall.
So the rose's petals shall not fall.
Red, red rose so clear and bright
Shall not fall without a fight.

Lauren Hunter (13)
Latimer Community Arts College

LIGHT POEM

Light, light ever so bright,
Shining in the dark, dark night.
Its calming rays shine brightly still,
Without this light you'd feel quite ill.
To feel the calmness of a wonderful breeze,
Light helps you see the birds and the trees.
When I feel sad light helps me conquer fears,
No more drowning sorrows, no more worries and tears.

Jamie Wilkins (12)
Latimer Community Arts College

Cows

Black and white patched cows walk lazily fazily,
Around the green grass field,
Chewing the cud
Like a horse would
Left, right, left, right,
Chewing,
Chewing.

They can be sweet,
But they can be demons,
Their moo can be deadly,
But mostly it's fine,
All I say is . . .
Never trust a cow.

Sophia Iannarelli (12)
Latimer Community Arts College

The Bike

Bike, the solitary bike.
Bike, the one by the wall.
Red, old, worn and frail,
Standing there beside the rail.

Birds fly by,
People pass,
But no notice is given,
To the bike on the grass.

As the day ends,
People scatter,
The bike still stands
All in a tatter.

Thomas Oldfield (13)
Latimer Community Arts College

TWO DIFFERENT WORLDS

As the world begins to wake
I hear the call of the morning quake
I spot the thin, tall spire of the parish church,
Calling, calling, calling with God's own special words.

I glanced to the right
At the developing building site,
An ugly place
Like the Devil's claw.

I saw out of the corner of my eyes
The majestic woodland,
A beautiful place
And home to so many animals.

It seems in this age and race,
Two different worlds are trying to bond together
But do not really get on.

Although we the human beings
Are trapped in the heart of it.
Yet we are the cause of it.

Chloe Swingler (12)
Latimer Community Arts College

WHO AM I?

I can be a dragon,
I can be a house.
I can be a football.
Who am I?

I can be a face,
I can be a cat,
I can be a leaf.
Who am I?

I can be white,
I can be grey,
I can disappear.
Who am I?

Have you guessed yet?
Yes it's me,
Look up high,
I'm a cloud.

Lindsay Appleton (12)
Latimer Community Arts College

THE JACK-IN-THE-BOX

Jump jump goes the jack-in-the-box
Laughter laughter as it pops up
As it pops up someone screams
Can't stop playing with it
Crying with laughter someone shouts 'Stop!'
So the jack-in-the-box stops going
Pop!

Jade Farrer (11)
Manor School

THE THIEF OF THE BATTLEGROUND

Guns are blazing, and many men are dead,
the fearless fight on, forgetting their pains;
they grieve for the friends, whose blood has been shed
and think of their anguish, losses and gains.

The mortar goes off, the shell hits the ground
the men that remain, look upwards in fear
as the dense mustard cloud, starts to surround
and panic sets in, as death becomes near.

In desperation, the soldiers take flight
and scramble for masks, in hope to survive;
their fear-filled faces, a harrowing sight
are suffused with burns, but onward they strive.

The men now are dead, their lives thieved by war
love, hope, lust and joy, they shall feel no more.

Adam Kemp (16)
Manor School

FISHING

Fishing is my thing,
I've done it all my life,
And when I fish,
I like to think about,
Cars and games and bikes.

I went on a Saturday and met a bloke,
That mimes,
He showed me how to catch a pike,
And how to cast a line.

Oliver Maitland (11)
Manor School

LOVE

Love is a many splendoured thing,
or so they say.
But is not the preconception of a
prosperous relationship false?
For venturing into this unknown
part of life is like becoming
a sponge: one moment you are
light and bouncy and then you
are weighted and immobile,
Complications drowning your mind.

The holes in love get bigger and
no matter how much you try to
patch them up, they won't go away.
The most acclaimed surgeon
could not mend the wounds of love.

Gina Heatley (15)
Manor School

ICE HOCKEY

Ice hockey is what I find interesting because I love to skate,
The sport that most people hate,
The speed and pace is just so great,
But the matches start all so late.

This sport comes from Canada,
From the great frozen lakes,
The ice is so cold it gives you the shakes.

This sport is so rough,
You need to be tough,
To compete in this sport you need all the stuff.

Ryan Jones (12)
Manor School

MY POEM ABOUT WRITING A POEM

A poem of no more than thirty lines,
Mrs Rich set the homework, to test our minds,
Will I write fiction or will it be fact?
Using my best English and lots of tact.
Five verses I'll write all with six lines,
And I'll try to think of verses in rhymes.

I've picked up my pen and my mind's gone blank,
That could be the fault of the Coca-Cola I drank.
The pressure is on, the words won't appear,
Have it finished by tomorrow? You can't be sincere.
To finish one verse I'd need a week,
Perhaps someone's advice I need to seek.

I went to my mum first and discussed all my thoughts,
She gave me some good ideas of weird sorts,
Dad was busy on the extension,
I've got to get this done or else detention.
No one else wanted to help me try,
Soon I'm going to sit down and cry.

Animals, holidays, all make good topics,
The only problem being, I've not been to the tropics,
Witches and wizards, it's nearly Hallowe'en,
Maybe some of the sights I've seen,
My little sister Kira would make a good story,
Which brother to use? Perry, Liam or Cory?

I'm really not sure what I'm going to write,
It's been a long day and even longer night,
I hope Mrs Rich will be understanding,
Kira's gone to bed and I've been evicted to the landing,
In one night thirty lines is a lot,
I wish, though, I could think of a really good plot.

Adele Bulmer (12)
Manor School

WHAT ON EARTH?

Earth planetariums possess strange things.
What are these ghastly, green objects
That are fed with a liquid substance?
Why do Earthlings attempt to communicate with them,
When they clearly don't know how to communicate back?
Maybe Earth creatures and green things are telepathic,
But to us they seem unintelligible and pathetic.

These things are fed once every Earth rotation
And seem to enlarge as time progresses,
They grow towards the light. They die with no sun.

Some grow tall
Some stay small
Others produce food which humans devour,
Bitter, sweet, salty or sour.
They don't seem to have any sex or gender,
They are neither male or female.

Earth-souls use the phraseology: 'petals' and 'leaves'
To describe particular parts of
these things' anatomy
Which we are yet to discover.
Are these dangerous
Toxic and harmful?

They have a sensational, strange, scented smell,
And have an amazing array of colours.
They make no sound, but move as the air blows around.
But to us they are a queer race.

They look like nothing on our planet,
So we have been studying them for a while,
And they might be inferior, but they absorb the same atmosphere as us
So we'd die out if we bred them.
On our planet we need CO_2 to survive.
We, as a superior race, want to stay alive.

Lucy De Friend (15)
Manor School

THE SCALES

Once I was her pedestal: I could do no wrong.
I would support her when emotions were firm.
Daily I would be her foundation before light broke.
A large slab, I sit on the floor near the water bowl,
It never produces such joy.
My forthrightness brought much joy, and life was sweet.

As time strained and sagged, life soared,
She screamed and spat against my curdled facts.
Two or three times a day her bitter insults attacked me.
Never did I falter, only truths did I tell.

Now jettisoned, as if I weighed her down,
I sit in the cheerless black.
I, the dishevelled, dishonest liar, make way for progress.
Ousted from my house by the credibility of digital,
But I still hear the cries of anguish!

Alex Ng (15)
Manor School

UNKNOWN LOVE

The love I'd always yearned for
Was always by my side.
Although I had not seen its beauty,
It began slowly blossoming,
Into the most beautiful, colourful flower in creation.
Slowly, silently and softly
We grew together and now; now
We are we, not just her and me.
In realisation of both our affection
Now when our eyes meet in a certain direction
It's not hard to notice or build up of tension:
It becomes hard to breathe, my chest becomes tight,
As tight as the leather face of a drum,
The drum on which my heart pounds,
Keeping its steady, predictable rhythm,
But skipping one beat every now and again.
Such a feeling cannot be expressed with a pen
Especially if written by insensitive men.
Nervous smiles are exchanged.
The brilliant white of our chattering teeth
Reflect burning desires that are yet to be seen.

Oliver Owers-Gibbs (15)
Manor School

THE WANDERER

He feels for his possessions,
Trapped amongst the rubble,
Screams of terror and pain,
Block the scavenger's thoughts.

He waits, listens,
Acts with caution,
As he hears the screech
Of metallic birds overhead.

He hides lying amongst death.
An authoritative voice rings out;
He is scared but unmoved
As he lets time and enemies pass.

This man, who is a fugitive
From his own country,
Lives a life of danger
And of immense suffering.

His ragged clothes and dim expression,
Explain his understanding of the situation,
And how the war has destroyed
The Wanderer's identity.

Adam Gayton (15)
Manor School

CARS

They come big and small,
Some are rounded, some are tall,
Three wheelers and fours,
All cars have two or four doors.

Leather and fabric seats
Air conditioning makes different heats,
Massive engines in all shapes,
Good cars have video tapes.

They come in all makes,
In limos you can make pancakes,
Rover, Porsche and Ford,
With these cars I'll never get bored.

Cars are red, cars are blue,
Cars go fast, if you want them to,
Music is another big thing,
Use this feature and have a sing.

Ben Munns (11)
Manor School

MY POEM

The stars are dazzling, the moon is bright,
The lamp posts are shining,
Through the night.

It's cold outside,
The trees are rustling,
The cars are zooming,
Down my street.

Chris Sinclair (11)
Manor School

CANOEING

Under the sun,
Canoeing is fun.
The water was gushing.
The canoe, it was rushing.
The floating is bumpy,
It makes you quite jumpy.
As you go over the weir,
You have to wear the right gear.
Rapids are scary,
Do you feel darey?
The water is cold,
So keep a tight hold.
When you turn, there's a water jet;
But watch out mate, you might get wet.

The rain was pouring,
Houseboats were mooring.
The wind was blowing,
And I was rowing.
I sat in my saddle,
Holding my paddle.
Wrapped up snug, in my warm life jacket.
The water made an awful racket,
Protect your head, wear a helmet.
Canoeing is fun if you can hack it.
The water's fast flowing,
And I do love going.
You should try it,
You might even buy it.

Michael Lewis (11)
Manor School

THE MILLENNIUM

We are all looking forward
To the next Millennium,
I wonder what will happen
To me and you and them.
Will all the clocks stop ticking?
Will computers get a bug?
Will the world stop turning?
I don't think so, I'm no mug.

I will carry on as normal
When New Year has gone,
The next day will be just the same,
Jobs still have to be done.

But I'll make the most of this one
And enjoy it all the same,
I'm going to a party to celebrate its fame.

Ashlee Stovold (11)
Manor School

MY DOLPHIN

Leaping high above the waves,
Flashing colours before my eyes.
Blue, grey and shimmering silver,
Showing off to fishermen.
The sparkling sea is her stage,
Dancing like a ballerina.
Swishing her tail,
Diving deep.
All this I see as I fall asleep,
My paperweight dolphin's secret life.

Victoria Commins (11)
Manor School

KITTEN

A friendly kitten,
As warm as a mitten.
It's like a child,
But wild.

I like its cry,
It looks at the sky.
Leaps in the air,
As I stare.

My kitten's black,
It climbs on my back.
It's also white,
It sleeps at night.

Kayleigh Manciocchi (11)
Manor School

AUTUMN

Leaves are falling on the ground,
Red, orange, green and brown.

Conkers dropping to the floor,
In ones or twos or threes or fours.

The bonfire burning, red and bright,
Its glowing flames shine against the dark night.

The animals hibernate in their homes,
The freezing cold attacking their bones.

Summer, autumn, winter, spring,
The seasons circle in a continuous ring.

Emma Saddington (11)
Manor School

FOOTBALL

Kicking a football around,
Is a lot better than listening to sound.

Football, you give it your all,
For 90 minutes you're no one's fool.

Scoring is so cool,
It is a lot better playing for your school.

Play on every Sunday all day,
Improves the game we play.

You take centre on the pitch,
You run all day it gives.

Daniel Marsh (12)
Manor School

LONELY

She stands in the corner of our living room,
Staring into space,
Mum says she looks like me,
Wonky and out of place!

I got her for Christmas,
But still she's standing there,
I wonder if she's thinking
'This really isn't fair!

If I could walk up the stairs
To be with the others,
We could be a family
With lots of sisters and brothers.'

In case you're wondering what she is,
She's a lonely little soul,
This is mini Tara,
My porcelain doll!

Tara Damon (11)
Manor School

MY POEM ON BARLEY

I have a dog called Barley,
She is a proper Charlie!
On her duvet she does repine,
Waiting for the time to dine.
For her dinner Barley eats,
Some yummy, yummy doggie meat.
Her toy is called King Kong,
And goes bouncy, bouncy, bong.
In the utility she is supposed to guard,
But does not bark very hard.
Her coat is liver and white,
With eyes golden bright.
A springer spaniel for all to see,
She is a 100% pedigree.

Jade Wiggins (11)
Manor School

WHY?

I sat alone in the corner
With tears running down from my eyes
People around are laughing
I just want to know why.

Is it because of my colour?
Is it because of my face?
People around are laughing
Just because of my race.

My father is a Christian
My mother is a Jew
People around are laughing
And calling me 'Hey you.'

I want them all to stop
Why don't they leave me alone?
People around are laughing
But all I can hear is a drone.

They've taken away my money
They've taken all my pride
People around are laughing
I just want to hide.

Katie Wilson & Jade Dixon-Winters (13)
Prince William School

THE FOX

The fox is very cunning
The fox is very keen
But every time he sees me
He's sure to think I'm mean.

The other day I had a plan
That I would be a hunting man
I'd load my gun for fire
And get what I desire.

The fox came around the tree
I'm sure he didn't see me
I'm going to kill him right here, right now
Here comes the blast . . . *wow!*

Oh my God what have I done?
I shot him with my dad's best gun
I've just realised this could mean trouble
Animal lovers could burst my bubble.

I hope that no one saw me
Or I shall feel quite poor
I don't know where to put it
I wish I never killed it.

The fox started moving and then started running
I jumped up with joy and thought it was stunning
I started crying tears of joy
As I knew I felt just like a toy.

Raymond Chambers (13)
Prince William School

IT'S OUR WORLD!

It's our world to keep forever,
So don't pollute it and we'll stay together,
It's ours to keep,
So keep it clean.
I dream of a world with golden moons and stars
That glisten in the night.
I dream of birds that fly together
In a wondrous flight.
These are not dreams, they are true life,
So respect our world and our world will respect us.
It's our life source forever
So look after it now
Or you'll regret it later.

Kirsty Neild (13)
Prince William School

THE DAY I DIED

The day I died was terrible,
I let out a great big scream.
After that it seemed like,
It had all become a dream.

Lying on the battlefield,
My life flashed before my eyes.
Then as I came to meet my death,
I looked up at the skies.

A friend of mine was ahead,
He shrieked out in hell.
The screaming stopped and then I knew,
That he was gone as well.

Leigh Middleton (11)
Roade School

REACHING FOR . . .

The light shines from across the water,
As though floating effortlessly
Guiding and enticing the vessels in.
The space that separates them,
Yet beckons him to reach out and grasp the magic.

An inaccessible focus for his yearning,
Gives definition to desire
Trying to reach for the past,
And wishing on a star that is out of reach,
Yet seems so close, is already behind him.

He attempts to use the moonlight
To defeat the endless tick of the clock
The irreversibility of time against a dream,
A dream doomed to fail.
He lived in the unreality of reality.

The American Dream has failed,
It has collapsed under a corrupt society,
Taking with it the dreams of the great.
Injustice triumphs, but life goes on,
It is better to have a dream than to be incomplete.

Louise Coombes (17)
Prince William School

DIANA

That was she, the girl who was my friend.
She looked at me with no enthusiasm,
Like a cold winter's morning.
Her lips so crimson,
and her teeth as white as the snow.
Whilst her rosy red hair,
shone in the light.
She could not look at me,
Just blankly stared at the floor,
with her eyes as green as the grass.
She broadly walked,
to her new-found friends,
and gave me no second look.
She moved with elegance,
and great posture,
Like a swan gliding across a lake.
She whispered to them,
with a look of guilt and all I could feel,
was hatred and pain.

Fiona Warren (13)
Prince William School

PEACE NOT WAR

Why isn't there peace, only war,
Just so they can score,
By claiming more land,
Why is this impossible to understand?

Why make war,
When you can have peace,
Why not be the one to cause it to cease,
Why not make peace?

Why cause all this distress
And this awful bloody mess,
This is in your best interest,
Put down your guns and rest!

Why not learn to agree,
Learn to love?
It's best for the people from whom you claim innocent lives,
Instead of all this war and strife.

Claire Solesbury (13)
Prince William School

SECRETS

Remote, a desolate scene, standing between life and
death.
Mysterious texture,
Powerful nature,
Forgotten times and a grave of memories.
An unearthly shadow fills the frame with gloom.
Lustreless, threadlike clouds barely cover the precious
moon.
A mass of metal,
Rusty and shattered.
A gloomy death, within life.
The saviour owl, the only fortunate creature living,
Dives, then passes over with an open mind and
glowing eye.
He knows its secret.

Claire Warren (15)
Prince William School

ANGER!

I'm stuck in a blazing fire and there is no way out,
Red is the colour I'm becoming.
I have an uneasy feeling in my chest,
I'm being hurt and hurt again and again.
It's like looking for a red bead when they are all purple.
I'm all steamed up and hot,
I want to hurt something, someone.

My anger is turning to hatred.
I cry out for help but no one blinks an eyelid.
The fire is burning me up,
My legs have gone.
I try to run from my anger but it keeps catching me up.
It's eating me up and there is no way back.

Lisa Snoxell (13)
Prince William School

DUSK AND DAWN

The dark, ebony, distant evening rests on the horizon
Night throws its cloak over the land
Bitter cold biting at the sky
Silent and mysterious the night waits for morning
Frost settles wherever it can

The birds chant and harmonise at the sight of the sun
The nightly frost melts into dew
The warmth of day takes over the night cold
Sunshine streams through the misty clouds
There is a soft humid silence in the air.

Sophie Dall (13)
Prince William School

UNTOUCHED IVORY

She stood alone
In a crowd
A strong blue aura surrounded her
She was beautiful.
Her golden curls tumbling over her
Smooth shoulders.
Her eyes of the deepest blue,
Like pools you could drown in.
Her lips the colour of the darkest rose
Her complexion as smooth as ivory.
Unaware of the world's suffering
She stands frozen in time
In the perfect moment.

Sophie O'Brien (15)
Prince William School

MY LOVE IS LIKE . . .

My love is like a rhyming poem . . .
it flows like a love-boat down the stream,
it's just like a flowing dream,
it's like a lightning bolt flying through the sky,
it's like a love-heart dazzling in my eye!

My love is like a rhyming poem . . .
it's slow and meaningful like the words on the page,
it doesn't matter about the age,
my love is like a sunset in the sky,
it's like a star twinkling in my eye.

Rachel Dunn (13)
Prince William School

THE SWAN

Swans are such elegant creatures,
They have so many pretty features,
They're snowy white and they don't bite,
Gliding gracefully across the river.

After winter then comes the spring,
Soon they mate and quickly bring
Sticks and moss to make a nest,
She lays her eggs and on them rests.

Sitting on the riverbank,
Till one day thankfully
She hears a crack of shell,
And slowly, one by one the cygnets fell,
Onto their downy bed.

Down to the river they soon go
To see their father and to show
Off their gliding through the water,
Two scruffy boys and a little daughter.

Tom Grace (13)
Prince William School

A DARK AND MISTY NIGHT

A flash of sharp and striking light
Appeared from the sky.
So high above the clouds
In funny little mounds.
Next, the city was darkened
As dark as could be.

Sharp and bitter
Like moonlit glitter.
Strange and white
As a dove in flight.
Drifting like a kite
In the cold and misty night.

James Rudkin (13)
Prince William School

ODE TO JOY

What is joy?
Joy is, sun, trees,
Frozen peas,
Happiness, light,
Fun and life,
Sand, sea,
Clean air.

Joy is plentiful,
Joy is where you look for it,
Joy is where the heart is.

Everyone has an inner joy,
Every girl and every boy,
From many, it rarely springs,
For many, it often flourishes,
Joy is the food of life,
And all of us it nourishes.

Philip Costin (14)
Roade School

CONFIDENCE IN FRIENDSHIPS

Confidence, confidence,
Is such a thing of pride.
It shows you stick up for yourself
And you don't run and hide.
It shows you are brave,
And shows you can do something,
And you are willing to save
Your friendship and your trust.

Confidence, confidence,
Is a good thing to have.
Its meaning is ability
And it shows you're a good friend to have.
It shows you are brave,
It shows you could do many things
And you are willing to save
Your friendship and trust.

Megan Boot (11)
Roade School

UNLUCKY IN LOVE

Love is an emotion
That everyone has known
It's just a shame
That it isn't always shown

Love is something
That picks and chooses
Sometimes your heart wins
And sometimes it loses

Love is something
That should grow day by day
February, March
April or May

You have to be careful
When love is involved
It doesn't mean every problem you have
Will suddenly be solved.

Hannah Maher (13)
Roade School

THE UNKNOWN LOVE

As he was walking towards me,
I could feel my heart beating faster than normal.
I felt all sweaty and scared inside,
He looked so nice in his cream, warm fleece.
His short black hair and his dark brown eyes,
Made him look so kind and sweet.
His smile makes me feel warm inside,
No one looks as cute as him.
As he walked past me,
The smell of him made me feel weak at the knees.

Days go by and I like him more and more.
I haven't spoken to him yet,
As I am scared of what he may think.
I'm really shy and think I'll make a fool of myself,
But he does make me feel warm inside.

Jennifer Gordon (14)
Roade School

LOVE MAKES LIFE

Love is a moment you cherish
Love is a thing you need
Love is a thing you feel around you
Love is a memory.

Love is the world moulded together
Love is a thing around forever
Love is a family's heart
Never failing but staying hard.

It will never leave you
It will never die
But fly up into the sky
And will be with you forever and ever.

Jennifer Duckett (13)
Roade School

THE SILENT SCARECROW

The silent scarecrow swaying in the wind,
Only ragged clothes, not neat and trimmed.
He stands there still every day,
Until the farmer takes him away.

The silent scarecrow standing there,
The trees are blowing, the hedges bare.
Some crows come and make fun of him,
They leave the crops, just make a din.

He must be lonely in the field,
But come harvest - what a yield!

Hannah Spotwood (14)
Roade School

BEDROOM

'Go and tidy your bedroom
Do it now or you will be grounded
This place is turning into a house of doom
Do it now or you will be pounded'

I think of every excuse
I've got lots of homework to do
I need a drink of juice
I might need to use plan number two

Thinking of this task makes me feel blue
I hear my mum screaming 'Go tidy your room'
There is such a lot to do
So I climb the stairs to meet my doom.

Daniel Whitlock (14)
Roade School

WINTER

Freezing cold on a winter's day,
Whoosh, whoosh,
Children all come out to play,
Whoosh, whoosh,
Animals start to hibernate,
Whoosh, whoosh,
Icy path and snowy gate,
Whoosh, whoosh,
This is on a winter's day when
Everyone wants to
Play . . . and . . . play.

Hannah Steele (12)
Roade School

THERE ONCE WAS A CAT

There once was a cat
And he sat in my lap.
He was white and fluffy
And he was very funny.

He used to wish
For a piece of fish.
It only came true
At quarter to two.

He loves his fish
When it's in a dish.
With a bowl of cream
And a nice dream.

He snuggles up to me
But I let him be.
Until he wakes up
Then it's time for brunch.

Hayley Creffield (14)
Roade School

HORSES

Horses walk
Horses eat grass
Horses can trot
Horses are nothing like humans
Horses are just one animal that can change one
Human's life.

Sarah Kennedy (11)
Roade School

LOVE

Love is a thing
that everybody needs,
it never annoys you
like wretched weeds.

It grows on you gradually
and will always be,
right by your side,
and clear to see.

Love is addictive,
like chocolate and sweets,
it's much more pleasant
than getting birthday treats.

Love is a dream,
known to all,
but now and again
love can be cruel.

But nevertheless,
you'll always get through,
the bad times you face
and your love will be true!

Amy Whittle (13)
Roade School

MY LITTLE BROTHER

From day to day,
Night to night,
I wonder what they think,
I'm scared of what they'll say,
I know they are my friends.

From day to day,
Night to night,
I'm teaching him new things,
He's learning new things,
Although it's step by step.

From day to day,
Night to night,
I lay in bed awake,
Worrying about nothing,
Apart from Ben.

Laura Bradshaw (12)
Roade School

LOVE

Love is like a dove,
Fluttering from above,
I wish I was in love,
In love like that dove,
That fluttered from above
And brought this special love.

Doug Mackenzie (13)
Roade School

TAKING A WRONG TURN

Darkness falls, and covers the land,
Everything is rotten and black,
So now what was once light,
Can never, ever come back.

The howling wolves of night are coming,
Searching for the evil in your soul,
Once they have found it, there's no going back,
Shrouded, with no escape, your heart turns to coal.

Just as black, and just as hard as mine,
Which has remained the same for years,
Soaked in remorse, pain and sorrow,
And children's young blood and tears.

Despair and sadness is all I have,
I am a renegade to what is right,
But right now, I'm a man without a cause,
A nomad imprisoned at the Devil's delight.

I have taken a wrong turn,
On life's twisted, deceitful road,
There's no exit, just a highway to hell,
No way out, of Satan's abode!

Lee Holod (14)
Roade School

WHY ME?

Everyone gets picked,
and I'm just left alone.
No one seems to care
If I'm on my own.
Even my best friends seem to leave me,
I haven't done anything wrong.

Their words act like they're throwing stones,
but none yet have thrown the crushing blow.
I try hard to fit in,
I suppose someone has to take the fall.
I keep asking myself,
Why me?

Everyone seems to have dreams,
I do, but I don't know what they mean.
Are they my future?
Or am I just going insane?
It's not fair,
The way people make me feel.
Can't they pick on something less real?
One day my wounds will heal.

Ryan Oakley (14)
Roade School

ODE ON LIFE

Life is like a flower, it starts from a seed
It can become a flower and it can become a weed
For it can develop slowly or quickly as it seems
Except it can be full of reality and it can be full of dreams.

Victoria Hayward (14)
Roade School

ANNA'S RELIEF

Relieved I am now,
That huge weight has left my shoulders.

They understand
They don't make fun,
I thought they would,
But I was wrong!

I was afraid to tell them,
Until one found out,
So I had to stop bad rumours getting about.

I should have told them sooner,
About poor handicapped Ben,
But now I am quite happy,
No need to cry or fuss,
Everyone is nice enough,
Even though they sometimes rush.

Benedict,
Oh, he doesn't care,
He's never embarrassed anywhere,
Ben the darling, I will love forever,
To me he is almost perfectly normal,
In every way that could possibly be.

Abigail Stanbridge (12)
Roade School

WINTER

The roads are slippy
It's icy and cold
A gale is blowing north, east and west
Oh! How I wish to be at home
By the light of the fire
With a mug of cocoa
All steamy and warm
A book to read
All old and worn
Curled up in an armchair
In a tight huddled ball
The roar of the fire
The purr of the cat

Outside the mountains are covered in icy frost
The trees are bare
Winter has its hold for now
But soon the spring will be back
The shining sun
And the laughter of children
Small echoes among the trees
Seem so far away
From this desolate and barren land.

Kathryn Johnson (14)
Roade School

THE GARDEN

The garden is a place for rest,
To relax while watching the world go by.
Listen to the birds singing,
The same routine every day.

Lots of flowers different colours,
Blues, purples, pinks and yellows.
Forget-me-nots, tulips, roses,
The same routine every day.

Nicola Swinney (11)
Roade School

ANNA'S RELIEF

Now the word is out,
Anna has no doubt,
That her brother has a big head.

In Anna's mind,
Is everyone's kind,
That her brother has a big head.

Anna's boredom,
Is locked in her room,
'Cause her brother has a big head.

Miranda for sure,
Is no longer a bore,
'Cause her brother has a big head.

As the word has spread,
Anna has a dread,
That her brother would be picked on.

Christopher Osgood (12)
Roade School

THE JOB INTERVIEW

I put on my shirt, I put on my tie,
I'm not nervous, I'm not shy,
I've waited for ages for this day,
Now I have forgotten what to say,
I woke up this morning in a sweaty hot sweat,
I need this job because I'm in debt.

I walked out the door, references in hand,
Then I walked along the golden sand,
When I got to my destination,
I went straight in for my interrogation,
They gave me the third degree,
I was so nervous I needed a wee,
I'm sure that my sweet talking did shine,
And the receptionist's job will be mine.

Adam Murby (14)
Roade School

BROTHERS

Some brothers are horrible,
Some brothers are a pain,
Some brothers even send you insane.

They can be nice,
They can be cruel,
They can be smart and often a fool.

My brother and I,
Fight all the time,
I can never trust him,
To stand by my side.

Kelly Lack (14)
Roade School

FRIENDSHIP/LOVE

They're smiling at me from a distance,
Where the sun always shines.
A cheeky grin, the sad puppy dog eyes,
It makes me want to cry sometimes.
Wherever I go, whatever I do,
I can't stop thinking of you.
You're tearing up my heart and soul,
I wish you felt the same.

I love the warmth when you surround me,
Your arms are closely wrapped around me.
Why can't we be more than friends?
It's driving me around some bends.
I just thought I would say,
I'm crazy for you.
In a strange little way
I wish you felt the same.

Your smile brightens up a miserable day,
You leave me speechless with nothing to say.
You give me hugs
In a sweet way.
The lovely smell of cold, frosty air,
Reminds me of you and your fuzzy black hair.
I wish you felt the same.

Gaby Knight (14)
Roade School

DISASTER AREA

My bedroom is always a tip,
In my quilt there is a big rip.
To see the state of my bed,
You'd think I slept on my head.
There's junk all over the floor,
It's so bad you can't open the door.
My mum seems to think I have rats,
That's why we have so many cats.

My brother won't even come near,
'Cause he's scared he will disappear.
Beneath the mountains of waste,
Where he once found some mouldy old paste,
From last year's wonderful dish
Of carrots, peas and fish!

When my mum tells me to tidy up,
I have to play on my luck.
'Cause the moment I dread,
Is when she looks under the bed,
And sees the mess,
With my crumpled dress.

She gives a very big shout,
And I'm told to 'clean it out'!
For this afternoon's guest,
Who thinks a tidy room is best!

Rebecca Hayward (14)
Roade School

SCHOOL POEM

I had better hurry, I'm going to be late,
Look at my uniform, it's such a state,
I get to the bus stop in a hurry,
I look like a mouse in a scurry,
I get to school, the bell rings,
I walk past a classroom where the school choir sings,
First lesson's history, to me it's a mystery,
Second lesson's dance,
Then to geography, doing a project on France,
Next it's lunch, where I have a munch
And hang out with my friends in a bunch,
Next it's double food,
But I'm not in the mood,
Two hours till home time, I can't wait,
But knowing my luck, the bus will be late!

Jenna Harrison (14)
Roade School

BYE

There's something cold and blank behind your smile,
Something was wrong,
You were in denial.
You were from a perfect world,
The world that threw you away,
That day you ran away.
A pill to make you numb,
A pill that made you dumb.
A pill to make you anybody else,
But all the drugs in this world
Could not save you from yourself.

Hannah Mead (14)
Roade School

THE SAVIOUR

The deep soul of light messed
With the darkened shadows of the night
And the meaning of life 'what'?
The question of the Saviour 'meaning life'
No meaning

With this meaning my eyes were glued
And my mind was stuck on the Saviour's face
The Saviour was a winner
The Saviour was a leader
The Saviour was dead.

With this thought my mind was screwed
The loss of the Saviour pulled me to the end
With my heart pumping with that one last beat
The Saviour was gone 'forever'
And the Saviour still 'no meaning'.

Harry Ingram (14)
Roade School

LOST

Lost in the forest
Scared and alone
No one to show
Where there is a way out,
Out of this terrifying blackness

Tall blackened trees sway
Against the dark star-studded sky
Frantic footsteps trample
On wet earth covered
In slippery wet leaves

Darkness envelops all around and
The panic rises inside
Running, running
Trying to escape,
Falling over stones on the ground

Icy winds scream past
Then blinding light illuminates
All the eye can see
Voices are shouting, screaming out
And I am safe.

Nicola Powell (14)
Roade School

TRAFFIC

There's no mistake,
I smell that stench,
It's that time of day again.
Time to sit back,
For the railway track,
Something blocks the road again,
And a standstill not for the first time.

Wet windscreen,
The leaking seam,
They have just been repaired
And the rain pours down, not the first time.

And all the drivers slam down their hands,
Open up and start their lunch,
Talk about who they'd like to punch.
Usual boys in the traffic jam.

Harsimran Samrai (15)
Roade School

THE LIFE AND TIMES OF A FLY

Here I am,
Buzzing around,
Trying to find
Some food on the ground.

When I get some,
I will devour,
Then bring it back up
Using my stomach power.

But my life is too short,
My dad lived just a week
And also there's humans,
It's me they seek.

Yes, they want me dead,
With their poison spray,
If that stuff goes in me,
It'll be my last day.

But what's this I see,
A blue square pad,
It just hit me, *ouch!*
Looks like I'm off to see Dad.

Sam Desborough (14)
Roade School

MEMORY LANE

This house is full of memories
Ones that mean to me
The parties and Christmas trees
That make me grin with glee.

My eyes fill up with tears as
I think back to years where
My family used to sit while
Watching the TV.

The cat used to purr when we
Stroked its soft fur.
The log fire burnt as the dog
Chewed its bone, when outside
The head fell off the gnome.

All these memories make me
Want to stay, but deep in my
Mind I know I have to go away.

But let's hope I will be happy
In my new home, it will mark
A new beginning from my
Family home.

Sophie Hillyard (15)
Roade School

I LOVE THE WAY . . .

I love the way your face creases up with laughter,
I love the way you get enthusiastic over everything,
I love the way you dance when you're happy,
I love the way you cry at sad films,
I love the way you want to be good,
I love the way you don't mean to be bad,
I love the way your feet tap to a jazzy song,
I love the way you can't whistle a tune,
I love the way your voice sounds when you're angry,
I love the way your voice sounds when you're not,
I love the way you always listen,
I love the way you love a good chat,
I love the way you worry over nothing,
I love the way you don't care about anything,
I love the way you try to explain things,
I love the way you keep it simple,
But most of all, out of all those things,
I love the way you love me!

Nicky Lloyd (15)
Roade School

OLIVER, MY LITTLE BROTHER

A brother is a menace,
Trying to annoy,
When you have your friends round,
He steals your favourite toy.

He thinks he's king of the world,
But Mum says he's not,
He goes into a rampage,
And then he won't stop.

A brother says he can have what he likes,
Even a new push bike,
When he says he wants a submarine,
Dad says he's living in a dream.

A younger brother is not all bad,
In fact, he's probably
The best friend I've ever had.

Becci Moss (12)
Roade School

DEATH

(This poem was written for my grandad
who died a few weeks ago. I wrote it on the
night he died to express my feelings)

Death will occur in every life,
Even though it causes pain, stress and strife.
People up there will look down and say,
Don't cry, missing us won't pay.
But we can't help crying like we're insane,
But please remember they were probably in pain.
Their bubbly spirit is still around,
Chasing the wind and leaves off the ground.
Their voice will softly speak,
Whereas they are as strong as a lion
                but before they were weak.
Think of them on a good time,
When you get sad, please remember this rhyme.

Lauren Dyer (12)
Roade School

Us . . .

Best friends,
Best friends never
Ever lie to each other.
So trustworthy,
Too good to be true?

True friends,
True friends are
Good for each other.
Close, like a rainbow,
Different but together.

Real friends,
Real friends are
Reliant on each other.
Only doors apart,
So close, so close.

Best friends . . .
You and me . . .
Us!

Laura Murdoch (11)
Roade School

Ben

As I walk into school,
Everybody looks at me,
I feel a fool,
And don't want to be.

Then everyone is sweet,
As I turn sad,
And it's just a treat,
That I feel glad.

Then I think of the times I've had,
Then of the times I have to be,
Then I feel so happy,
Everyone is nice to me.

Then as I get home,
And see my brother,
He's soft and sweet,
Just like a feather.

Ashley Woodward (12)
Roade School

ANNA'S SECRET

I'm just so relieved,
And glad and pleased,
I'm rid of secret Ben!

The secret I had in my mind,
Which I wouldn't let outside,
Has gone.
And I was wrong,
'Cause everyone's been so nice!

I'm just so relieved,
And glad and pleased,
I'm rid of secret Ben!

Debbie's been caring,
And I've been daring,
By telling everyone about Ben.
Even Emma's been nice,
Which is quite a surprise,
I'm just glad I'm rid of secret Ben!

Louise Wroblewska (12)
Roade School

THE BOY WAS BORN

The boy was born
my life has changed
but one day it was not very nice
as I was looking at a price
in the post office round the corner.
She came in the door
and I fell through the floor
as Miranda came in the door.
I felt so poor
as she saw
my brother in his pram.
I was so relieved at school
the next day
as people liked me more
but then I bumped into a door.

Claire Ratledge (12)
Roade School

ANNA

I'm glad of my sense of relief
because I was getting sick to the back teeth
of my secret inside
I was trying to hide
I'm glad of my sense of relief

I thought they'd laugh but I was just
being daft
Even Emma is nice
and that's a surprise.

Kelly Hayle (12)
Roade School

ANNA'S HAPPINESS

I'm happy now,
oh yes I am
because they understand
my baby brother
Benny boy
is different from the crowd.

I should have told my
friends before,
I thought that they would
laugh.

I told my friends that
Ben was handicapped.
They gasped and were
surprised.

Now everybody knows
my secret's out
I'm glad the truth's been
told.

Hannah Fraser (12)
Roade School

LOVE CAN DO ALL SORTS OF THINGS

Love can do all sorts of things,
Love can break your heart
And destroy your life,
Love can do all sorts of things,
Love can mend your heart
And make your life happier,
Love can do all sorts of things,
Just be patient,
You never know what might happen.

Zoé Bassett (11)
Roade School

TO MARS AND BACK AGAIN!

When I grow up the world will be a better place,
It will not matter if you are black or white in the face.
People will not call out racist names
And will stop playing mind games.
No fights or destruction, poverty and no world wars,
People will now fight for a good cause.
No one will die of the dreadful cancer
And we will not look at the rain in the shape of acid but a dancer.
Pesticides will go,
Organic fruit, worldwide, will grow.
Space cars will somehow run on sea water,
Instead of the normal cars our world they slaughter.
Holidays in Skegness no more,
But to Mars it is a legal law.

Amanda Hoppe (13)
Sir Christopher Hatton School

THE ANIMALS' FUTURE

The future holds a dreadful fate,
for all wild animals who await
their fate of death and extinction
because of the human race.
No more lions, no more tigers
but just fur rugs and trophies and
animals' heads in gamekeepers' huts.
No more animals, no more elephants
they've all be used for ancient
Chinese herbal medicine.
Don't forget the creatures in the sea,
they too have a death destiny
from fish-nets and fishermen and
fishmongers and *you!*
Well you wouldn't like it if they
were eating you.
Cute little sea horses, gigantic whales,
deluxe dolphin swimmers are all
getting killed,
as well as lions and tigers and gorillas
the list goes on, it seems almost endless.
So I hope this poem has changed your mind,
about the way you think about all wild animals
for they too have a future.

Jennifer Whitby (13)
Sir Christopher Hatton School

FUTURE

In the future technology will grow,
Just like the seeds that people sow

I hope it will be good,
I know it should

War and hunger will stop,
Because technology will be on top!

Nuclear bombs will be gone,
Then the world can get along

The planet Earth is the place to be,
For the millennium wait and see!

Greg Knight (13)
Sir Christopher Hatton School

THE FUTURE

In the future will there be peace and tranquillity,
What will happen to human ability,
Will we ever understand the brain?
Will the millennium reduce stress and strain?
Will we ever find the end of the universe?
Will people believe any ancient curse?
Will every disease and sickness be cured?
Will our future be frightening,
Or will our lives pass like lightning?

Siân Louise Cairns (13)
Sir Christopher Hatton School

IN THE MILLENNIUM

In the millennium
I hope we'll see a change
We'll travel up to space to see what lies in store
And journey to the depths of the ocean for a holiday,
To see the dolphins dance and play,
Will be able to fly in special cars that hover in the sky,
They'll be so great in years to come we'll all be flying high.

In the millennium
I hope we'll have a clean environment,
For the animals of tomorrow,
Because if we are not careful their lives will be full of sorrow,
Animals and plants will slowly die away,
We must try to save the animals of tomorrow
And save the environment today.

In the millennium
I hope we'll have world peace,
There'll be no fighting in the world,
Everyone will be at ease,
There'll be no bombs or nuclear wars
And everyone will be free to do as they please,
So no one will have to suffer anymore.

Rebecca Fenner (13)
Sir Christopher Hatton School

THE FUTURE

The future is disaster, full of guts and gore,
And just around the corner is a giant Third World War!

There's atom bombs strewn all around,
Explosions here and there.
The sound of twisted screams of pain
Are splitting through the air!

The latest weapons big and bold, can cut through
Flesh and steel and bone
And though you think you're safe at your station
You're in line for decapitation!

Machines for firing weapons,
Machines for building them,
Machines for tearing off your limbs,
When will this ever end?

But think about the good things, the flowers all around,
But the only plants are trees and they are holograms.

So all in all the future doesn't look too promising,
But the thing you must remember, just one tiny little thing,
Machines will fight the humans and I just bet they'll win!

Jason Reade (13)
Sir Christopher Hatton School

MILLENNIUM

I often wonder what the future will bring
Will it be such a wonderful thing?
Singing and dancing on millennium night
Lights in the town shining ever so bright.

I often wonder about poverty and war
Memories of what I've heard and saw
Will things get better? Will things get worse?
It's almost like an innocent curse.

I often wonder about remembering the past
Just how long will the future last?
Will it be good? Will it be bad?
When it comes I'm sure I'll be glad.

I often wonder about the homeless on the street
Aches and pains running through their feet
Nowhere to wander, nowhere to roam
No centrally heated house to call their own.

The children of today will be adults of tomorrow
Will poverty, war and homelessness be one big sorrow?
Let's try and make the future as good as we can
Because one step for today, is one step for man.

Jasmine Thomas (14)
Sir Christopher Hatton School

FUTURE VOICES

We should have been prepared
We should have asked for help
But no . . .

We just sat there
They came in their hordes
Destroying our armies
Killing
Leaving death behind them

Now we are their slaves
Now they rule our world
But there's hope . . .

Reinforcements are arriving
The protectors are coming
Freedom . . .

David Caswell (13)
Sir Christopher Hatton School

THE FUTURE

T   he world and universe,
H   ave been destroyed.
E   volution has destroyed them.

F   lames lick up the buildings,
U   nder the sea fish are dying, oil has leaked.
T   orturous spikes protrude from the walls,
U   ranium leaks freely from power plants.
R   emains of humans strewn about,
E   volution has destroyed!

Chris Pape (13)
Sir Christopher Hatton School

THE FUTURE . . .

The future is coming, the future is near
The future is coming, coming this year.
The future is technology controlling the world
The future is technology being hurled.
The future is happy, children playing in the park
The future is light sitting in the dark.
The future is a song with bright joyful words
The future is the sky filled with birds.
The future is the sun melting an ice-cream
The future is a planet that has never been seen.
The future is me, the future is you
The future is all our dreams come true.
The future is a book with open pages
The future is the world with different ages.

Laura Sharman (13)
Sir Christopher Hatton School

THE FUTURE IS

F   uture is computers.
U   nlike the past the future is bright.
T   he future will be an excellent place.
U   nexplored territories.
R   evolutionising the world as we know it.
E   ventually the world will end.

Karl Maxwell (13)
Sir Christopher Hatton School

ROBOTS, ROBOTS

Robots, robots,
They'll do your little jobs,
Robots, robots,
They'll fix your bits and bobs
Robots, robots,
They'll do it in half the time,
Robots, robots,
If you ask nicely you might get a dime,
Robots, robots,
They're hard to fix,
Robots, robots,
If you try you'll get in a mix,
Robots, robots,
They'll take over your lives,
Robots, robots,
Soon you'll be living in hives,
Robots, robots,
They're not worth the trouble,
Robots, robots,
You'll just pop the bubble,

Robots, robots,
Are everywhere,
Robots, robots,
They've now got hair,
Robots, robots,
They've taken over the Earth,
Robots, robots,
Now they're even giving birth.

Emily Fisher (13)
Sir Christopher Hatton School

A VOICE FROM THE FUTURE!

These voices, these voices,
I hear them, they follow me,
They talk and tell me
About the future, our world.

He tells me, 'Believe in prospect,
Prosperity will come.
Follow your heart.'
The future, our world.

You will be an adult,
Our next generation.
Politicians will rise.'
The future, our world.

Technology is the key,
With computers,
Our lives will change.
The future, our world.

It could be good,
It could be bad,
The meaning of future goes on.
The future, our world.

It's all a big mystery,
Only time will tell,
The future lies within,
The years of the 2000,
The millennium.
The future is our world.

Kerry Hand (14)
Sir Christopher Hatton School

FUTURE VOICES!

What is the future?
There may be no future.
The human civilisation may be no more
Or man may live to experience the
next millennium.

Our children are the future voices
But what does the future maintain?
The repetitive ticking of the clock,
Which is a leap into the future.

We will adapt to a new opening
An opening to lifelong understanding.
This is our world,
We do what we want.

Charlotte Dunkley (13)
Sir Christopher Hatton School

FUTURE

In the future we might live on
the moon,
Or we'll still live on the Earth

We'll be in cars that fly high,
Above the sky

Spaceships will be bigger and better
And aliens will be found,

Our future is good, our future is
Bright, our future is about
Flight

Luke Armstrong (13)
Sir Christopher Hatton School

FUTURE VOICES, SPACE SHUTTLE

They advance down the corridor,
Pride and fear crushing them.
Such heroes of this colourful Earth,
What will come?
They stand in line,
Scrutinising the monumental space shuttle.
They say their goodbyes
And float . . .
Into an abstracted, shadowy wonderland.
Fantasy ripens into reality!
They stride, nearing the massive opening
To a world, a non-gravitational hallucination
The door shuts,
And locks them into oblivion
The moment of severity,
The countdown . . .
An explosion of commotion,
The beginning of the end!

Rebecca Daldy (13)
Sir Christopher Hatton School

FUTURE

F   lying cars past the stars,
U   seless humans sleeping in bed,
T   aking time off to go to Mars,
U   sing things never used before,
R   obots working all day long.
E   ndless fun because the future is here.

Jade Baldwin (13)
Sir Christopher Hatton School

THE FUTURE

Why oh why am I the only human?
All I see now are robots,
There's no one to talk to and
no one to play with.

Computers do everything,
from typing to loading.
There's nothing for me to do.

When the sun runs out,
robots sleep.
It's the only time I am safe.

So why oh why am I the only human?

Holly Parker (13)
Sir Christopher Hatton School

THE FUTURE

People laughing at horrid jokes.
Flying cars which give off smoke.
Smiley faces that show a frown.
Kings and queens don't wear their crowns.
New inventions which are no use.
Silly bands with names like Moose.
Computers try to rule the world.
Straight lines now are changed to curled.
Unhappy children with no food.
Nice comments are classed as rude.

Adele Pride (14)
Sir Christopher Hatton School

FUTURE VOICES

The girl walked through the deserted city,
Alone.
The darkness crashing down on her,
Thinking.
Will she be the hit of the millennium,
Or is she going to be a nothing?
A dark hole in the universe
She keeps on walking, not knowing her destination.
Suddenly, she comes to a dead end.
A high wall?
She can't see what is behind it.
Is this a sign?
She hears a noise.
Rustling,
She runs,
Her red leather shoes clicking on the drab grey stones.
A second later she gets hit!
A sharp pain!
A screeching noise.
She hears a cry
And suddenly she blacks out.
She lies there,
Her limp body covered in dark clothes.
Her red leather shoes,
They are the only things that shine in the darkness.
She will not have to worry about her future now!

Munisha Odedra (13)
Sir Christopher Hatton School

FUTURE VOICES

The warning has been and keeps on coming
but stops at intervals.
We wait in our shelters
Hoping everything will stop.
We know it won't
but we can always hope.
We wait in terror for something to happen.

The ground tremors.
Something's happened
Or has it?
I go outside
To see what it was.
Nothing.

I was surprised but happy.
It might have stopped.
I go to the shelter to tell my family.
I got in just in time
as a loud noise followed me.

I am relieved
that I am safe.
Something has really happened this time.
Why is God letting us do this to our world?

Jenny Cook (14)
Sir Christopher Hatton School

FUTURE VOICES

Our planet
A different world
Operated by computers
New, bizarre fashions.
We will not understand them.
Fresh, unnatural inventions
Like electronic blackboards that do not need chalk
Favourite holidays, arranged by 'Lunn Pluto'
Visiting Venus, with day trips to Mars.
Air on Earth, clean and pure
Not a trace of car fumes and litter.
Modes of transport, bikes and petrol-free cars.

More people live to 100
Cigarettes and tobacco will not exist
More diseases cured.
We will mature into adulthood
By then, money will grow on trees.
So no one will have to work.

People, riding horses in the sky.
Death will come and, well,
The end of the world.

Sarah Meleleu (13)
Sir Christopher Hatton School

THE VOICES OF THE FUTURE

We should have been ready,
For the end,
We should have had defences,
But no . . .
We thought we were invincible
They proved we were wrong,
They walked over our army,
They were twice our size,
Huge lingering bodies,
Causing chaos.

Four long limbs,
Two for balancing,
And two for holding their weaponry,
They walked around like they owned the place,
But we will prove them wrong,
Soon, we hope, our back-up will come,
And we will prosper,
They will not defeat us,
They will not break our determination,
To walk free again on our planet.

We will get revenge,
We'll refuse to work,
Cause riots,
Start to rebel,
They can't hold us forever,
We'll fight to the death
With these weapons that we've made,
Those humans think they're top,
But here we are,
To get back what's ours.

Brendan Clarke (14)
Sir Christopher Hatton School

SOLDIER'S PRAYER

My heart's in my ears,
I can hear it like a loud scream.
I'm inside a cocktail shaker,
Will it ever blend me in.

I look around me.
There are faces of fear, hope and despair.
We are all huddled together,
Like particles in a solid.

Every wave I sense,
I'm presented with drops of the deadly enemy.
The sea.
Like bony fingers tapping on my hat of gold, to urge me on.

'I'm a soldier, I can put up with it for Britain!'
Is the chant that keeps me going,
When my best friends are shot to the ground,
And the thought of death is racing through my mind.

Up I wake every day.
Expecting to hear the yells of agony,
And the ongoing bullets of death.
I feel like one of *Satan's* messengers,
All I have in my mind now is kill, kill, kill!

I try to look beyond this graveyard
And hope and pray there is victory around the next corner
I will hopefully turn.

All those lives lost.
Families torn apart.
Souls were left without hearts in 1939.
Peace for the future.
No more pain.

Sarah Forster (13)
Sir Christopher Hatton School

WHO KNOWS?

I look into the future and the only thing I see
is questions, questions, questions,
no one knows the true answers.

Who knows what the future will hold
When all the children grow?
Will they be the same as us
Or will we be Stone Age?

To think our technology may grow old
It is hard to understand
Should the world become one
To end all suffering and pain?

What will happen after we've gone?
Will the ozone layer grow?
Will all our animals die away?
Will technology go too far?

Will the world end in a bang
or a huge earthquake or fire?
Will civilisation destroy itself?
Will the robots rule the world?

Has mankind done enough
To protect the beauty of the land?
Or will skyscrapers and dense cities
Change the way of life?

Have our ancestors done wrong
By only looking out for number 1?
What will the next generation
Grow up to be?

How do we tell what it will be
We can't - we must wait and see
Tomorrow, next year, who knows?
Who knows what the future will hold?

And all that's left to say is
See you in the future.

Irene Lewis (13)
Sir Christopher Hatton School

FUTURE VOICES

You are now entering the future,
Be warned it's not a pretty sight,
It's full of murder and crime,
Cities are chaotic,
Towns are overcrowded,
People are running,
Running for their lives.

Files are lost,
Banks closed,
Hospitals have even come to a standstill,
The Millennium Bug has arrived.

You can't see it,
You can't feel it,
But it's there,
Waiting to feed off of more electricity,
The year 00,
Is waiting for us!

Lindsay Hillburn (13)
Sir Christopher Hatton School

LIGHTS, CAMERA, ACTION

The hall was full of people talking aloud
The curtains went up, the hall was silent
No place to hide.

The lights came up
The spotlight was on me,
I began.

The people in the audience
Just faces, no emotions.

Just me on an empty stage,
Nobody to rescue me,
Nowhere to run from my fears.

There was a loud roar from the audience.
I slowly walked off the stage
Giving a sigh of relief

     It was all over.

Sarah Spreckley (12)
Sir Christopher Hatton School

FUTURE VOICES

We hide in the draughty bunker,
Drowsy and agitated.
We are silent,
Listening.

Everybody is tired,
Daring not to sleep.
We are waiting . . .
Waiting for something to wait for.
We are all waiting in fear,
The future is our fear.

There is an intense, powerful sound,
Another
Then another.
We are alert,
Will this be the end?

I close my eyes,
Fighting back my tears.
How did this happen?
It is not our fault,
Yet we are the victims of the suffering.
Eventually we will have to surface,
To face our uncertain future.

Robert Bradshaw (13)
Sir Christopher Hatton School

FUTURE VOICES

The world is dying,
Our future, passing
As each day goes by
Our future shortens.

One giant puzzle
Mysterious, ongoing
When will it end?
Nobody knows.

One giant risk
Mysterious as it seems
Not knowing what the future holds
Or what it may bring.

Kunaal Arora (13)
Sir Christopher Hatton School

FUTURE VOICES

Millennium,
Parties, streamers and fireworks,
But what will really happen?
Will the Millennium Bug hit?
Is the world about to end?
Everybody seems so happy,
But will our happiness come crashing down?
Ruining all of our plans,
The millennium, a disaster,
Our hope for a great new century fading,
The world as we know it, gone,
Or will a new century bring new hope?
No more wars,
Or suffering,
Will aliens land?
Will we find new planets?
Will our world completely change?
New generations bring new ideas,
Change the world,
Stand up to be counted,
Be the future voices.

Joanna Loomes (13)
Sir Christopher Hatton School

FUTURE VOICES

Here we are,
There it is,
The new, our new, everyone's new planet.
The vast land,
The great rivers and lakes,
The unpolluted air,
Everything is great.
Millions of us left,
Our old planet Earth.
I look out,
Out into space,
Seeing all the other spacecraft,
Coming into land.
The flat land,
The mountains in the background.
The children wander off,
But the parents don't mind.
Nothing can happen,
The scientists and builders,
They came.
The burglars and criminals,
They didn't.
A life of peace,
Is what they want,
But is it all,
They will get.

Michael Soper (13)
Sir Christopher Hatton School

THE MILLENNIUM

The Millennium Stadium,
I look forward to the future,
The mammoth Stadium built for the World Cup,
I look forward to the future.

The eye of London,
The future's sight,
The Cyclops of the city,
The future's sight.

The giant Dome,
I look forward to the future,
Its upright structure blinds you,
I look forward for the future . . .

George Shipman (13)
Sir Christopher Hatton School

THE FUTURE

The world is dying away slowly,
Nothing left to see.
The plants and trees are losing their strength,
Computers ruling free.
People now are extinct,
Robots king and queen.
The universe is growing larger,
No more space left for me.

Computers rule our time, our work, our space,
Technology working for us.
New cures for diseases have come,
Cancer no longer a threat.
NASA organising space trips for us,
People living in space.
Education's been taken over by computers,
Programmes to suit every need.

Daniela Sacco (13)
Sir Christopher Hatton School

THE MILLENNIUM + A DOME

The millennium . . . good or not?
I don't think so!

You see the Millennium Dome.
The white superstructure like an upside down
cereal bowl.
You walk in.
You look around, amazed, gaping like a fish
that hasn't seen anything before.
The clock starts ticking down.
It takes an eternity, like a turtle running
a marathon.
You run around all excited, like a runner who
is running the 100meters.
The bells of Big Ben toll twelve.
Each dong echoes around the Dome.
It goes silent.
So silent you could hear a pin drop.

Is that it?
What . . . a waste . . . of time!

Joseph Roberts (13)
Sir Christopher Hatton School

Gooooooooodniiiiiight

I call 'Goodnight' to my mum as I go to bed,
Creak, creak, the sound of the stairs sends shivers down my spine,
I open my black door and step into the darkness,
I turn out the light and try to sleep.
Gurgle, gurgle, thump, thump,
I reach under the bed and I feel rubber,
I've never felt that before!
I feel a finger grip my hand,
I try to break free,
Can't, grip too tight,
I try to scream but nothing comes out,
It's pulling me under and under,
Squelch, squelch, squelch,
Help, I need help!
Muuuuuuuuuuuuuuummmmm . . . !

Sarah Underwood (11)
The Ferrers School

Exterminate!

I am an alien from outer space
I will come down on your Earth and invade you.
I am green with a silver eye.
I eat flesh, brown flesh with freckles.
I have never been on your Earth before.
I have never seen you people
But I have seen people who I am going to eat up.
Beee, beee, beee, beep.

Fiona Higgins (11)
The Ferrers School

JURASSIC PARK II

Scurrying the jungle floor,
Eating food more and more.
The diplodocus, hiding from hunters,
While the saurapod blunders.
Also the stegosaurus shows off his colours,
But in the sky it thunders.
But there is something everyone fears,
Something that would give you tears.
The remains of a dinosaur,
Attacked by a T-rex or more.
The giant reptile gives a great roar,
That scares the life out of a dinosaur.
He chases after the big dinosaurs,
Tracks them down and pushes them onto the floor.
Bit by bit he rips them apart,
All the way down to the heart.
Now I'll say 'Bye' to the dinosaurs,
As after the 'accident' there will be no more.

Richard Stuart Avis (11)
The Ferrers School

STAR WARS

Boba Fett saw some aliens fighting
so he looked them up in his alien book.
Green grans with green eyes.
Supersonic slugs with slimy tongues,
Micro mayhem as mini monsters fight.
Trying fire from fierce mutated snakes.
The ultimate chaos.

Adam Harris (11)
The Ferrers School

EARTH AND SPACE

E   arth looks so small up here in space,
A   nd the stars look so big,
R   ight out in space it seems so dark,
T   ry hard to keep the excitement in but it just bursts out,
H   appy that I'm going to the moon,

A   t the tip of my fingers are planets,
N   ear the moon,
D   ark turns to light in the brightness of the moon,

S   tars shining in the dark sky,
P   ieces of asteroids flying by,
A   spacecraft's in the sky,
C   ircling through the air
E   nding our flight in space.

Carly Tebbutt (11)
The Ferrers School

MY BROTHER

Shin basher
Computer crasher
Quick eater
Likes Beefeater
Lousy at Poker
Good joker
Slow sleeper
Brother beater.
My brother
There is no other.

Paul Dix (11)
The Ferrers School

LIVING IN MY HEAD

I went to sleep with a monster in my head.
Yes, it was a big, slimy, ugly-looking thing,
With four heads, seven fingers on both hands.
Three feet and five eyes.
It was a phenomenon.
I suddenly woke up, the coast was clear.
I went back to sleep and there it was again.
I just couldn't get it out of my head.
There it was just staring at me.
It pinched me and blew its stinking breath at me.
It was horrible and disgusting at the same time.
It told me it needed the loo,
Just think of all that goo.
I wish it could go away
And then, it vanished.

Kathryn Lusk (11)
The Ferrers School

THE RAT

A rat is a disgusting creature
It is a black ball of hair with eyes and legs.
It nibbles, giggles and wriggles its way around.
Its tail is a long thin string with lines on it.
It lives in a smelly and disgusting sewer.
It's a fat pig that always eats trashed food
Its body is like a rotten potato,
Its teeth are like yellow rotten bananas
Its head is like a soggy balloon
It is a disgusting, smelly rat.

Daniel Murgatroyd (11)
The Ferrers School

THE HUGE UGLY LIME GREEN THING

Ugh! I saw it today
It's disgusting, revolting
It has two tentacles with two eyes on each
Dripping slime, making a puddle
Teeth as sharp as a bread knife
I thought it was just normal, lying there all alone
Now I doubt that because it glowed
I tried to pick it up and put it in the bin
But when I tried it jumped and ran away
It was bedtime now
'I don't want to, I'm scared.'
I hoped it would go away.
But who was I kidding, it was gonna be there every day.

Martin Fortescue (12)
The Ferrers School

SPACE JOURNEY

S   ilence as I
P   ace myself
A   gain we shall meet
C   ount those stars
E   clipse in the east.

J   ourney to space
O   ver the moon
U   ranus, I can see it
R   ain down on Earth
N   eptune I can see you
E   arth you're miles away
Y   es I'm on a space journey.

Lauren Peters (11)
The Ferrers School

SPACE

Space, I have always wanted to visit space,
To see the world from a high view.
Lots of people have told me about it.
They say it's a round ball of fire.
I wonder what it is like.
Are there aliens?
Are there monsters?
Oh I wonder what it's like.

If there are aliens, what will they be like?
Will their heads be like mouldy spaghetti?
Will their bodies be like soggy toast?
Will their legs be like sausages?
Will their mouths be like chainsaws?

Aaaahhhh! I can't think about it.

If I meet a monster what will I do?
I'll scream and shout,
As I stare into shining metal eyes
I'll feel dizzy, I'll fall to the ground.

I don't think I want to go.
Meet the monsters,
Meet the aliens.
I think I'll stay at home,
In my nice cosy bed.

Samantha Newell (11)
The Ferrers School

MONSTERS UNDER THE BED

'Goodnight Mum!'
I say as I go up to bed
I get into my room and close the door
I turn out my bedside table lamp
I snuggle up into my bed
Then I hear a gurgle and a burp.
I jump up and turn my light on
I start to call for my parents,
My heart is beating like a bass drum
I look under my bed.
There it is, a big, fat pink-haired seven eyed monster
I go towards my door and it jumps out towards me
It grabs hold of me with its slimy green fingers
I scream and try to escape
But it is no good.

Laura Hammond (11)
The Ferrers School

THE NEW WORLD

S   is for space, the marvellous new world!
P   is for panic, what might go wrong?
A   is for aliens, the unknown creature,
C   is for a celebration when we go to the moon.
E   is for everything, I want to see everything.
S   is for scared, I am very scared.
H   is for hurry, we must get going.
I   is for important, an important mission.
P   is for peace. We bring peace.

Lisa Humphreys (11)
The Ferrers School

IT'S ROUND, IT'S ROUGH AND STICKY TOO!

Sitting down nice and snug,
When someone really starts to bug,
'Ow my eye,'
'It's stuck in my hair,'
'To be quite honest I really don't care,'
Yells the person who interrupted the film.
'It's round, it's rough and sticky too,'
'It went in my mouth,'
'I'm gonna be sick in the loo!'
There's a round light coming up the aisle,
It shines in my face,
It scans around at others,
Angry faces and squinting eyes,
'Get that light out of my eye,' someone calls.
The light stops.
Slouched down in the seat is a little boy,
He has brown hair and lots of freckles,
He has a worried face,
But a mischievous smile,
Held in his hand is a piece of popcorn!
The boy puts the popcorn back in the box,
He tries to smile as if only joking,
But the guide won't have it,
The boy slowly stands up,
Angry faces stare at him,
He is followed by several people,
Actually the whole audience,
He runs faster and faster,
'Aaaarrrggghhh!'

Kathleen Clark (11)
The Ferrers School

CONFUSION

Memories shattered,
Thoughts, questions,
Why? How?
Will I ever see him again?

Lost friendship,
Lost love,
Nothing can make up for him,
Nothing.

Loneliness,
Depression,
Words can't express my feelings,
Thoughts replaying - 'He's really gone!'

If I could have it any other way,
I would.
It's not fair!
It's just not fair.

Melanie Clare Smith (11)
The Ferrers School

SPACE

S   pace is big and full
P   lanets are misty and dull
A   liens are lurking around this place
C   urrently this place is called Space
E   arth, yes my home, let's go back.

Michael Steel (12)
The Ferrers School

THE FUTURE

In the future it will be different,
No cars but electric flying machines.
Half the world's former population,
Will be living on the moon,
There will be frequent alien attacks.
The sky will be covered in
Thick smog like burnt cotton wool.
But the world is worried.
The little people in the bright orange suits
Are worried.
There's an asteroid coming,
Soon the world's population will be down to 0.

The asteroid has struck,
Everybody is dead.
The score is now,
Asteroid 2. Man 0. Dinosaurs 0.

Sam Cole (11)
The Ferrers School

IN THE FUTURE

In the future bunny rabbits will rule the world,
And little green men from far away,
Will be our masters and we will be pets.

They will put us in cages,
Which will be in zoos,
We will be wildlife.

Money will not count,
And leaves will be like gold,
And then humans will be gone.

Michael Lord
The Ferrers School

GROOVY CHICK

My name is Duigy
and I like a bit of boogie
I think I'm funky
but yet punky
I like all the men who care for others
but they do completely the opposite to my brothers.
I am a groovy chick
when it comes to making tricks.
I'm rather like my mother
when I give out some bother
I like to sing and dance
when I've only got the chance.
So if you see a funky punky groovy chick
then be warned it's the Duigy chick.

Siân Duignan (11)
The Ferrers School

THE HEDGEHOG

Tiggy is a hedgehog
She lives under a shed
She scuttles in the grass
curls up in the leaves
She creeps out, when it gets
dark to find insects.
Soon she will have babies to feed.
The babies have arrived!
No prickles yet,
they lie with their eyes closed
while Tiggy feeds them.

Emma Wildman (12)
The Ferrers School

A PUFF OF MAGIC

Puffs of smoke
Mysterious myths
Houdini, Daniels,
Copperfield.
Coin tricks,
Card tricks
Sleight of
Hand.
There's a puff of
Smoke.
Houdini just made
A great escape.
Now it's my turn,
Poof!

Richard Adams (12)
The Ferrers School

STRANGE BUT TRUE

He's a strange big lad,
with a scrunched up face
sorry-eyed and mad.
He plays the drum bass,
curled over his drums.

He beats out a tune,
until the rhythm comes.

The other day
he went out to play.
He made up a tune
that was dead cool.

Kristina Harlow (12)
The Ferrers School

WINTER'S EFFECTS

Winter's frosts are sweeping in,
To deprive our country of warmth and light,
Ending our day and announcing the night.
Jack Frost has settled on the ground,
He has been dancing through the streets not making a sound.

When the glittering snow falls,
Songs of laughter fill the air,
From excited children throwing icy snowballs,
Whilst the snow is getting tangled in their clothes and hair,
The snow is so white and fluffy,
But then it turns into hard frozen ice and starts falling heavily.

The wind is howling,
With force and fury showing no mercy.
Thunder is approaching a rumble then growling,
Lightning is flashing a warning then striking.
It's tearing out trees like a dog rips up grass,
Windows smash smothering people in glass.

Still the daunting horror goes on,
The pain is getting stronger and stronger,
Gales of spite getting longer and longer.
Snowballs have turned to the size of a clenched fist,
The number of deaths has turned into an enormous list,
The pain and torture some people survived,
Is amazing really after all this happens yearly!

Hannah Collins (11)
The Ferrers School

THE SCHOOL TRIP

The dreaded school trip,
On the bus kids,
'Bob stop picking your nose,'
'Sir, he kicked me,'
'John don't kick Tony.'
Are we ever going to go?

'Sir I've forgotten my bag.'
'Go and get it, Alice.'
'I feel sick,'
'Tough,'
'I want my mum,'
'We haven't left yet.'
Are we ever going to go?

'Sir, she pulled my hair,'
'Don't,'
'Now *silence!*'
'Silence what a wonderful thing.'
'Sir . . .'

Joe Balfour (12)
The Ferrers School

ALIENS

A   liens are squashy
L   egs that wobble
I   'm scared
E   yes are so big
N   ot very nice.

   I'd never thought I'd see an alien.
   But now I have I know they are around.

Nikki Hammond (11)
The Ferrers School

REVENGE

Crash!
Oh no, I've smashed the vase,
Mum will kill me,
Lock me up and torture me,
Murder me, get a professional killer onto me.
Quick!
Tidy it up, where should I hide it?
Under the stairs,
In my dad's shoes,
In a bush,
Behind the tele?
Should I hide it in the strawberry flavoured jelly?
I know!
The perfect place,
I'll put it in my sister's room.
I'll blame it on her.
I've been meaning to get back at her,
For giving me a black eye.

'Lauren!' my mum yells,
I giggle to myself,
Revenge is sweet.

Jack Addis (11)
The Ferrers School

SHOPPING

If I go shopping with my money,
I feel really good!
Especially if it's really sunny,
Eating lots of junk food!

When I'm buying all I can,
I feel really nice!
Especially if I get a tan,
And buy at a really good price!

If I set out to spend some cash,
I feel all warm inside!
Afterwards to the park I dash,
Down where the bandstand lies.

Though I like to shop 'til I drop,
I like taking some money home too,
When I start I just can't stop!
I know I can't, how about you?

Zoë Johnstone Smith (11)
The Ferrers School

PEAS!

I hate peas
I think they are yuck
But my mum always says
'You must eat them all up.'

I'll say no
And I really don't care
Even if she shouts
'You stay on that chair.'

Lisa Dunn (12)
The Ferrers School

The Song Of The Whale

A long mournful cry echoes in the empty ocean,
A whale is singing, a whale is alone,
No family to accompany her,
just the fishes that swim around her fins.
She is crying, no one can see that,
the ocean disguises her everlasting tears.
She hopes the waves will wash away her sadness,
but it is no use, she is all alone.
Her family has been destroyed.
Evil men with big weapons killing innocent whales.
What is the world coming to?
Whales are for living in the free open ocean
being one of the world's greatest features.
Not lipstick for our greedy faces.
No family of whales
No whale
No whales.

Abigail Barnett (12)
The Ferrers School

Untitled

My brother is a dork
He mumbles when he talks,
He's slapped me round the head,
kicked me on the leg.
That's why I hate my brother.

One of these days,
He's going to pay
for what he's done to me.

Charlene Hicks (11)
The Ferrers School

MIDNIGHT

Midnight, I lie in bed,
Nothing to go to sleep for,
Everything to stay awake for,
I listen to the noises of the awakening night.

I hear the owls sing their song of beauty,
I listen as the nocturnal animals scurry along outside,
I see the moonlight creep through the curtains,
I listen to the noises of the awakening night.

I creep out of bed, the floorboards creak,
Something stirs . . .
. . . A bat on the window awakening from its rest,
I listen to the noises of the awakening, never-ending night.

Now I lie in bed, as fatigued as the next person,
Nothing to stay awake for,
Everything to go to sleep for,
I've seen the mysteries of the night. (Have you?)

Natalie Longley (11)
The Ferrers School

MY HOLIDAY

It was freezing cold,
And I was really fed up,
And soaked to the skin!
I remembered the fantastic holiday in Spain,
Roasting hot weather, clear blue sea,
Boiling beaches and a clear sky,
Now it's all a memory.

Louise Murphy (11)
The Ferrers School

SCHOOL

School can be fun
School can be annoying
School can be exciting
School can be upsetting.

Nobody likes school when they get told off
Or yelled at especially when they get yelled at
For no reason at all.

I like school when we go on school trips
I like school when it's time for lunch.
I especially like school when I'm playing with my friends
I like school even more when I'm waiting for my bus
To go home to my cosy bed.

Chrissy Marshall (11)
The Ferrers School

CHOCOLATE CAKE

Yummy yummy yummy,
This will burst my belly,
It feels so gorgeous in my tummy
I scoff it while I'm watching tele.

Yummy yummy yummy,
In my tummy,
choccie cake,
choccie cake,
In my tummy.

Susan Tester, Nathan Taylor & Georgina Taylor (11)
The Ferrers School

THE ENGLISH ROOM DOOR

The brown door to the English room door is like stretching an
elastic band and letting it go,
You could get your finger trapped in it,
Nobody knows.
You could get locked in,
You could get locked out,
But something will happen to you,
without a doubt.
Maybe your clothes will rip because of the door handle,
or it will catch alight
like a flaming candle.
Nobody knows
that's for sure
what's in store for you
from the English room door.

Lauren Gow (11)
The Ferrers School

ASTHMA

Out with friends
Having fun
Messing about
Having a run
Asthma strikes
Cannot breathe
Reach for inhaler
Give it a shake
Press the button
Hold it . . . wait!
All better.

Alyson Brown (11)
The Ferrers School

THE CRY

As I lie there in silence,
I can feel the frostbiting wave of air that has encircled me.
The lacy violas dancing in the breeze,
making faces, evil faces.
They are crying out to me,
It feels like the whole room is spinning.
Something is under my sheet,
My heart fills up with anxiety,
I scream and scream but no one can hear me,
It is hopeless,
I am at death's door.
Help!

Emma Macavoy (12)
The Ferrers School

THE SEA

The sun, beaming down on the blue bed of water,
The waves, crashing against the sand
glittering like stars in the midnight sky,
The seagulls' shrill cries across the salty sea breeze,
Children's laughs as they are being buried head to toe in sand,
Suncream being rubbed on sandy legs and arms,
Snoring dads under newspapers,
The sound of ice-cream trucks, with children racing after,
Families packing away ready to leave the sea for another day.

Sophie Brown (11)
The Ferrers School

THE HUMAN RACE

The human race, all over the place
Taking over the world.
With its massive buildings
And choking fumes.

It's expanding day by day
It's expanding night by night
It glows in the distance
A shining leading light.

It's a leading light in the distant future
For souls looking for work.
Yet poverty is still among us
And some are left alone.

James Taylor (12)
The Ferrers School

THE CAT

In a bundle of marmalade-coloured fur,
She lies peacefully, with a soft purr,
Curled in front of the fire, cosy and warm,
Wrapped in her owner's arms.

She stares out of the window, at the stars silver and bright,
Stretching out her paws with great might,
Her ears pricking up at every sound,
Such as hearing the neighbour's hound.

After the long day she falls asleep,
In her small, furry heap.

Claire Willis (12)
The Ferrers School

THE WONDERERS OF THE NIGHT

I wonder what's outside in the dark,
All I hear is a dog's vicious bark.
I look out of my window and down the vacant street,
Then as if from nowhere I hear my lonely heart beat.

I wonder whether night will ever end,
And in the morning I've got this bed to mend.
Lying here uncomfortable, silent and stiff,
Also in the morning I've got to meet Biff.

I wonder if anybody is awake,
And then I don't know why but I begin to shake.
Is it cold in here or is it just me?
Can I get to sleep? Let's try and see.

I close my eyes and hope for the best,
Then there is a slight breeze coming from the west.
I begin to dream of magic long and deep,
And so there I am in a long magical sleep.

Max Barnett (11)
The Ferrers School

A WILD HURRICANE

A wild hurricane is vicious and terrifying
Strong and fast it rides through cities
Like they are tinfoil.
Careless and hungry sweeping houses off the ground
A hurricane is dangerous but beautiful to see
If you could go into the eye it is lovely to be
Destroying homes and wrecking lives.

Chris Kitson (11)
The Ferrers School

HAWK

Majestically he swoops and soars,
A mile up, there are no laws!
On a thermal, higher he rides,
Far above the turning tides.

But then in a meadow, near a house,
Out comes the nose of a fieldmouse.
Then with keen eyes, he looks below,
And the mouse will never know!

Down he dives in a stoop,
Suddenly he does a loop!
He tumbles down! Through the air!
And still the mouse just doesn't care!

Three metres up! His wings flare,
This is such a frightening dare!
Talons close. Head lowers. What a thrill -
The hawk made a kill!

Adam Simons (12)
The Ferrers School

DEATH

I wonder what is after death,
Where will we be left
Will we be left in hell
Where we won't be treated well?

Or will we be left in heaven
Where everything is quiet and still?

Or is there really nothing?
Who can really tell?

John Hogan (12)
The Ferrers School

THE MIDNIGHT MANSION

No one goes in,
No one comes out.
From the top of the hill
You can hear people shout.

Lightning bolts soar,
Thunder roars loudly.
And outside the gates
An old wolf strolls proudly.

Some have seen ghosts,
Others have not.
People see vampires, werewolves,
The lot.

Doors slam loudly,
Curtains blow wildly.
And if you listen carefully
Faint voices whisper mildly.

The mysterious house
Stands alone on the hill.
No one goes near,
And no one ever will.

Jacob Underwood (11)
The Ferrers School

DETENTION!

Go into humanities, 'OK homework please,'
'Um, my dog chewed it up.'
'Yeah, yeah, *detention!*'

Walk into maths, 'I'm collecting in homework.'
'Miss I didn't have any,'
'Yeah, yeah, *detention!*'

Rush into German, 'Homework everyone,'
'I couldn't understand it.'
'Why didn't you tell me? *Detention!*'

Walk moodily into English, 'It's already late,'
You guessed it
'Detention!'

Happy it's PE 'But no kit for the third time,
Here we go again,'
'Detention!'

Well, what a day,
6 hours school, 10 hours
              Detention!

Richard Bird (11)
The Ferrers School

CATS

The cat is a beautiful animal
Pouncing on its food
Sometimes happy sometimes sad
Always changing its mood.

The lion is another type
With its majestic mane and tail
When catching its prey
Never does it fail.

Look at the tiger
With its lovely sleek black stripes
Ever so still and quiet
When prowling through the night.

Here comes the cheetah
As fast as the wind
Never stopping once
Except when the light of day is dimmed.

The way they jump
Then land on their feet
The way they purr
And how they keep their fur neat.

I love cats
So should you
We've got a black one
Now that's very new.

Erin Ardis (11)
The Ferrers School

COMPUTER GAMES

As I turn on my console
Insert the game and watch the video roll,
Driver, Ninja and Metal Gear,
They're so real it's as if they're here.
My favourite console, PlayStation,
The reason for this is because it's *fun!*
The story of PlayStation has just begun!

Ben Prentice (11)
The Ferrers School